Praise for *Reality-Based Leadership*

"An entertaining read, every chapter has an 'a-ha!' moment. Be a follower of Cy Wakeman's insights and solutions, and drive amazing results in any profession, industry, or company culture. Keep this essential reference for leaders at your fingertips!"

> —Victor Susman, chief operating officer, First National Merchant Solutions

"Cy Wakeman's energetic *Reality-Based Leadership* message is compelling and genuine. Her real-life experiences combined with her mastery of relating those experiences will captivate and influence readers. Her quick-wit key points will become memorable 'Cy-isms' in the workplace."

> —Diana M. Mehochko, president, First National Merchant Solutions, LLC

"Cy Wakeman provides the reader with an exquisite guide for developing individuals and the teams they lead. *Reality-Based Leadership* is chock full of marvelous resources and practical advice on building contemporary organizations that are able to thrive and weather change. This is a must-read for anyone committed to developing a truly successful and vibrant organization."

> —Geraldine Bednash, CEO, American Association of Colleges of Nursing

"Wow! Cy Wakeman's *Reality-Based Leadership* is an excellent, heartfelt, humorous, wisdom-filled, butt-kickin' leadership book! Cy has an amazing way of exposing the drama and stories to get to the soft underbelly of reality. She helps leaders recognize our limiting beliefs and challenges us to change our mindsets. As a general engineering contractor for 30 years, I am just learning to lead first and manage second, and love that I now have the wisdom and tools to recognize and capture the opportunity in every challenge."

> —Mary A. Larsen, president, Stormwater Specialists, General Engineering Contractors

"Read *Reality-Based Leadership* more as a testimonial to success rather than as just another theoretical business book. Cy Wakeman is not suggesting concepts here—she has lived what she writes. Cy understands that business operates in real time and is played out every day on the competitive pitch. And those who communicate expectations, hold people accountable, and continuously drive teams to higher and higher performance are richly rewarded. *Reality-Based Leadership* should inspire you to stop making excuses and have the courage to be successful, by first holding yourself accountable and next creating a culture of accountability inside your company!"

> —Doug R. Wilwerding, president and CEO, The Optimas Group, LLC

"Cy Wakeman is the Queen of Real. Her message to get over your bad self and lead is perfect for today's crazy business organizations that are steeped in self-righteous indignation. Got an issue? Get a tissue and move on!"

> —Lisa Harper, former CEO and chairman of the board, The Gymboree Corporation

"Insightful and practical. Cy Wakeman's unique, direct, and colorful approach provides a road map for leaders to drive accountability and empowers talent to achieve extraordinary results. This book is full of practical advice that I was able to put to use immediately!"

—Anne Wignall, senior vice president, human resources,
    Liberty Bank

"In *Reality-Based Leadership,* Cy Wakeman takes us on a journey of understanding how we as leaders are accountable and that, quite simply—there are no excuses. Own our vision, inspire our teams, drive results. *Reality-Based Leadership* provides the reader with Cy's straightforward, no-nonsense wisdom and great humor, a combination that has helped transform the leadership results of those who have worked with her. She provides a much-needed wake-up call to leaders everywhere."

—Scott Focht, Institute for Career Advancement Needs

"Cy Wakeman helps us understand that the 'facts' are not always as they seem. Reality-Based Leaders liberate and motivate others to understand self and colleagues. Everyone in the organization is empowered to be productive and successful, individually and collectively, achieving extraordinary outcomes with seemingly good ordinary people."

—Timothy M. Gaspar, dean and professor, the University of
    Toledo College of Nursing

"Cy Wakeman's book delivers a powerful message. The bottom line—this is required reading for all leaders!"

—Russ Olson, president and CEO, Liberty Bank

"Cy Wakeman turns the tables on conventional wisdom by showing you how to rise above the noise of interpersonal conflict. *Reality-Based Leadership* is a playbook on how to thrive in challenging times and lead your organization to breakthrough performance. Cy provides step-by-step instructions on how to have life-changing conversations and be the change you want to see in others. I know. It worked for me and it will for you too."

—Tim Singley, senior manager of operational excellence, Ingersoll Rand University

"The critical growth of business today is good leadership—this book hits the target. Its practical format is easily applied to every leadership challenge."

—Caroline Bailey, third-generation Gallo family and owner of Premier Growth, The Business of Family™

REALITY-BASED LEADERSHIP

Ditch the Drama, Restore
Sanity to the Workplace,
and Turn Excuses into Results

Cy Wakeman

Foreword by
Larry Winget

JOSSEY-BASS
A Wiley Imprint
www.josseybass.com

Published by Jossey-Bass
A Wiley Imprint
989 Market Street, San Francisco, CA 94103-1741—www.josseybass.com

Jossey-Bass books and products are available through most bookstores. To contact Jossey-Bass directly call our Customer Care Department within the U.S. at 800-956-7739, outside the U.S. at 317-572-3986, or fax 317-572-4002.

Jossey-Bass also publishes its books in a variety of electronic formats. Some content that appears in print may not be available in electronic books.

Library of Congress Cataloging-in-Publication Data

Wakeman, Cy.
  Reality-based leadership : ditch the drama, restore sanity to the workplace, and turn excuses into results / Cy Wakeman ; foreword by Larry Winget.
      p. cm.
  Includes bibliographical references and index.
  ISBN 978-0-470-61350-4 (hardback); ISBN 978-0-470-87521-6 (ebk);
  ISBN 978-0-470-87523-0 (ebk); ISBN 978-0-470-87525-4 (ebk)
  1. Leadership. I. Title.
  HD57.7.W3355 2010
  658.4'092—dc22

                                                    2010020676

Printed in the United States of America
FIRST EDITION
HB Printing   20 19 18 17 16 15 14 13 12

I dedicate this book with love and gratitude

*to my mother, who taught me the true meaning of
Amazing Grace—surround yourself with enough
amazing women in your life and you will be graced . . .*

*and to my dad, who taught me to always succeed
in spite of the facts . . . the beginnings of Reality-Based Leadership*

CONTENTS

FOREWORD   xi
by Larry Winget

INTRODUCTION: Calling All Leaders   1

PART ONE: FIND PEACE AT WORK   7

1 You Are the Source of Your Suffering—and That's the
Good News   9
2 If You Argue with Reality, You Lose (but Only 100 Percent
of the Time)   19
3 Would You Rather Be Right, or Wildly Successful?   35

PART TWO: RESTORE SANITY TO THE WORKPLACE   47

4 Lead First, Manage Second   49
5 Play Favorites: Work with the Willing!   69

Contents

6 Change Is a Fact of Life—Get Over It! How to Bullet-Proof
Your Employees   83

PART THREE: LEAD YOUR TEAM TO RESULTS   103

7 Opinions No Longer Count—Actions Do!   105
8 Stop Judging and Start Helping: The Golden Rule of
Teamwork   125

Conclusion The Reality-Based Leader's Manifesto   141

APPENDIXES   145

Appendix 1 Alignment Survey   147
Appendix 2 Self-Test: Managing Versus Leading   149
Appendix 3 Feedback Frame   153

NOTES   155
ACKNOWLEDGMENTS   157
ABOUT THE AUTHOR   161
INDEX   163

FOREWORD

I have never met Cy Wakeman. Strange, huh? Usually the Foreword of a book is written by one of the author's buddies. But that's not the case here. Her editor sent me her book to read for a cover blurb. If I had read it and hated it, I could have said so, or I could have said nothing. I didn't need to say something nice to make her feel good or to sustain our friendship. I didn't owe anyone anything on this one. So I opened the book with little expectation and no pressure to enjoy it. To my surprise, I read the whole thing in one sitting and found myself saying "Yes!" and "That sounds like *me*!" So I happily wrote a blurb and sent it to the editor because I genuinely liked the book. Wait. That's not exactly true; I loved the book. Which is a bit odd for me because I hate most business books. It's true. I've read more than 4,000 books in the past twenty years. That's right: 4,000. I don't know anyone who has read more books than I have. And most of the books were crap. A few were pretty good. Then there were the rare few that were outstanding. This is one of those outstanding books.

Why would I say that? What makes the book outstanding? It's real. Of course the other books were real too: real idealistic, real nice, and giving real bad advice not even remotely tied to the real world. Most were also real boring. Cy's book isn't idealistic. It isn't even all that nice. It's real world with real advice: no pie-in-the-sky BS here. It also isn't boring. What more could you ask for? How about this: this book is well written. It's compelling. It's honest. It's a fun read. It isn't some stupid parable. And it makes you think. *Bingo!* For me, that is the ultimate test for a book and that is what makes the book outstanding: it makes you think. Oh yeah, here's another thing I like: it makes you uncomfortable. That fits my whole approach, so that's probably why I like it so much.

I am the trademarked Pitbull of Personal Development® and World's Only Irritational Speaker®. It has always been my goal to make people uncomfortable in both my speeches and my books. I love to metaphorically slap people and have them flinch from the sting of my words. Then once I have their attention, I reel them back in with common sense, facts, logic, and humor and then give them a solid plan for changing. I have done it in the areas of personal development with my books *Shut Up, Stop Whining and Get a Life* and *The Idiot Factor*; in the area of business with *It's Called Work for a Reason!*; in the area of personal finance with *You're Broke Because You Want to Be*; and in parenting with *Your Kids Are Your Own Fault*. Each book delivers a healthy dose of discomfort that I hope makes you take responsibility for your current situation and encourages you to take action on a simple, realistic plan for improvement.

That is exactly what Cy has done in this book on leadership. She makes you uncomfortable by pointing out the mess our businesses are in and pointing the finger of blame in the face of one of the major causes: leadership. She allows you to assess your mistakes and then—this is the best part—gives you solid, commonsense, doable actions that can turn your mess around. She holds a mirror up close in your face and forces you to accept your role in your own success. She whispers in your ear the excuses you have been giving yourself about why you aren't doing as well as you think you should be doing. In other words, she kicks your butt and leaves you better off for it!

This book is not for those who love to blame the government, the economy, coworkers, or the changing world we live in. It's not for those who want everyone to love them and all they do. It's not for those who never want to be criticized. This book is for people who are willing to draw distinct lines between right and wrong and acceptable versus unacceptable behavior. It's for leaders who are willing to do the right thing instead of the popular thing and understand that their job is about getting results. It's not about doing well when everything is in your favor, but about doing well regardless of the hand you are dealt. Cy is so right to call her approach "Reality-Based Leadership," because that is exactly what it is based on: reality!

This part of a book is called the Foreword. It is designed to get you interested in reading the book. I hope I have been successful in doing that. But understand that this Foreword makes little difference in your results. Read the book. Pay attention to what Cy has to say. Learn some stuff. Change. Because it's what you do afterward that really counts!

July 2010   Larry Winget

REALITY-BASED
LEADERSHIP

INTRODUCTION

Calling All Leaders

If I ask you what drives you crazy at work—what holds you back from being an amazing leader and producing extraordinary results—chances are you won't have to reflect very long before coming up with an answer. Frustration is at an all-time high, and the responses I get to this question generally fall in one of two categories: people and circumstances.

The circumstances: sky-high customer expectations, the rising cost of doing business, increased regulation, the recession, the pace of change, budget cuts, and being asked to do more with fewer resources.

The people: whiny, high-maintenance employees with a sense of entitlement where their motivation and accountability ought to be, who prefer creating drama to getting the job done. Add undermining peers and unenlightened bosses, and it's jerks and idiots everywhere you look.

It's enough to send you screaming into an early retirement. With these obstacles and impediments, what are the odds you will make your numbers for the year, much less put an end to the suffering and find a little peace at work?

If you believe that leadership is tougher today than it was in the past, you're not alone. For the past eighteen years, I've worked with top executives and organizations who are seeking to thrive in difficult times. My clients range from nonprofits to global conglomerates; banks to agricultural organizations; universities to government agencies. You're right that we are facing challenging times in the business world today. Allow me to make a prediction: We will continue to face challenging times in the future.

Here's a reality check: We are living and working in dramatic and demanding times, but that is not our biggest problem. The source of our pain is the absence of great leadership that is based in reality. Poor leadership practices—past and present—are being exposed for what they are under reality's harsh glare. In the relatively recent past, tons of capital, rapid job creation, fast profits, and high stock prices covered for a multitude of sins, but the bottom line is, current leadership methods are not working, and it's time we admitted it.

A recent Gallup poll showed that 71 percent of employees are disengaged to the point that they consider quitting their jobs about once a day.[1] That's nearly two-thirds of the employee population. It may sound like a crazy number—and it would be if these employees were actually quitting. The truth is much worse: they're continuing to report to work and collect a paycheck, but mentally (and emotionally) they are clocked out. Our worst performers spend their days bitching, moaning, and whining (I like to say they're out driving their BMWs—bitching, moaning, and whining). Our best performers become self-righteous and judgmental. Most nurse a suspicion that their circumstances are sick, wrong, or unfair. Instead of engaging with reality, they argue against it, focusing their efforts on a battle they will surely lose.

As leaders, we are not helping. We talk more about our people than we do to them. We judge, and when we are judging we are no longer serving, leading, or learning. We can't expect others to add value when we don't. We spend too much time with our worst performers, and we don't reward our best. We over-manage and under-lead, trying to control people rather than connecting to them and developing their potential. We blindly hope everyone will show up tomorrow with a better attitude without taking measurable steps to ensure that it happens. It's no wonder drama—not peace—reigns supreme in most workplaces.

Human Resources can only address the symptoms of the problem—never the cause—because HR is, at best, several steps removed from reality as it plays out, day to day, in your office. HR's role is to protect the company and to serve the employees, not to fill in the gaps left by poor leadership.

The worst part of all this? Instead of getting the results we want, we end up with reasons, stories, and excuses for why things didn't work out—leading to more drama, disengagement, judgment, and ineffective leadership.

If you are a leader charged with finding a way to inspire that 71 percent of disengaged people, take heart. There's hope. Most people feel stressed at work because they spend the majority of their time, usually unconsciously, reacting against their circumstances instead of moving forward productively, without time-wasting, morale-killing defenses, excuses, or complaints. Your circumstances may not be negotiable, but your suffering is.

The future belongs to the leader who is able to change the way people think and perceive their circumstances, the leader who engages hearts and minds. But before you can be that leader, you have to change your own mind. I can show you how.

After decades of consulting to leaders around the world, speaking to hundreds of thousands of frustrated leaders, I've developed a philosophy I call "Reality-Based Leadership." It is a model for ditching the drama, restoring sanity to the workplace, and turning excuses into results. Most leaders are no more than a few courageous decisions away from extraordinary success, and the first is the decision to stop holding on to strategies that are no longer producing results for you.

Reality-Based Leaders quickly recognize and radically accept the reality of their situations and efficiently channel their (and others') energy toward optimizing results. Better yet, they learn to anticipate changes and capitalize on them as opportunities—without drama or defensiveness. What Reality-Based Leaders know is that great leadership is simple, but it's not easy. Even when it seems circumstances are against them, they choose how to react, and their reactions set the tone for everyone else.

By becoming a Reality-Based Leader, you will rid your organization of needless drama and insanity, replacing these drains on time and energy with peace, sanity, and most important, results—regardless of your circumstances. This book is divided into three parts, each of which builds on the one that went before. I'll show you how to transform your approach, one step at a time.

Part One: Find Peace at Work

You will

- Discover the amount of resources wasted on drama in your organization—and reclaim them for productivity
- Learn to distinguish between drama and fact by asking a few simple questions
- Find peace as you stop believing in your own stressful stories

Part Two: Restore Sanity to the Workplace

You will

- Begin to spread peace throughout your organization by making drama politically incorrect

- Learn counterintuitive ways to win people over
- Set bold new expectations for employees
- Discover a new way to coach people that rewards personal accountability and demands action

Part Three: Lead Your Team to Results

You will

- Find out why much of conventional wisdom on leadership is just plain wrong
- Find out how to apply Reality-Based Leadership principles to teams, to break through resistance and conflict (without playing referee)
- Harness negative energy for positive ends
- End excuses, editorializing, and judgment so that your office will become the one where everyone—including you—wants to work

Throughout the book, I supply real-life examples, diagnostic tests, and innovative tools that you can begin using immediately to great effect, dramatically changing your perspective about your possibilities.

These changes are not optional if you and your business are to be leaders in the new world. They will not be effortless to make, but they will free you from the frustrations and barriers you face at work and transform you into a Reality-Based Leader with the ability to liberate and inspire others. Your circumstances will not change; you will—first your thinking, and then your life. I've helped more than 150,000 people on their way to becoming Reality-Based Leaders. Read on if you want to join our revolution.

PART ONE

Find Peace at Work

Peace at work may strike you as an indistinct concept or a distant dream, but it's neither. Not only is it possible to have peace at work, it's essential to peak performance. In order to grasp it and bring it to life in your organization, you must first comprehend its opposite: drama.

Drama may seem to come from a variety of external sources—chief among them, other people and situations over which we have no control. But in Part One, I show you the surprising truth: most of the drama in our lives is self-created. I explain why that's so and how to begin to change your mindset and behavior in ways that help you increase the peace in your office. It's essential preparation for becoming an effective Reality-Based Leader.

1

You Are the Source of Your Suffering — and That's the Good News

One of the reasons leadership seems so tough right now is that a lot of focus and energy are dissipated on drama—gossip, judgment, resistance, and complaint—instead of productive, proactive work. When this is true in your organization, you feel you're working harder than ever before, and yet you don't get the results you want. Your frustration is high and your energy low. But it doesn't have to be this way. In this chapter, I help you assess how much of your and others' energy is being wasted on drama. I also discuss drama's main components and causes and why you should ban it from your office. Peace comes with the end of drama.

Suffering Is Optional: Stop Arguing with Reality

We all face the occasional setback or frustration, but suffering is optional. If you are suffering and peace is elusive, consider this counterintuitive idea: your mindset—not your circumstances—is the source of your pain.

Here's how it works: Think of a time when one of your coworkers received a promotion. You may have made an instant judgment such as, "That's unfair! What about me?" Such a judgment taps into deeply held—possibly unconscious or unquestioned—beliefs, such as:

"I am always overlooked while others are rewarded."
"I do all the work while brownnosers like her get all the glory."
"I spend my time doing my job, not playing politics—that's why I have yet to get a promotion. It's all about sucking up."

These ideas quickly coalesce into a story: "She is so political she was able to brownnose her way into that position without ever really accomplishing anything. I produce results, but around here only politics matter." Your judgment, plus your beliefs, become your story, and that always equals *stress*. Congratulations: you now work for a company that is unfair, political, unrewarding (at least for you) and promotes people for the wrong reasons. A company you have created in your own mind.

When things get tough at work, most of us think about quitting or moving to a different company. But I'm here to tell you: It is most likely your thinking—not your job—that needs to change.

When you look at the facts of the situation I just described, all you know for sure is that a coworker was promoted. The rest is your own fabrication, based on untruths such as "I never get chosen." (Yet, you were chosen for your current job over all other candidates, right?) Because of your judgments and beliefs, you pout instead of being helpful and adding value.

If, rather than judging and storytelling, you embraced reality, you would note that a promotion occurred and do the appropriate thing in such a situation: congratulate your coworker, offer to help in any way you can, and resolve to learn from her how to deliver what the company values. You'd be high on professionalism, low on drama, and investing in better relationships and mutual support in the future.

In this book, I relate many stories about the leaders I coach. But first I give you a personal example, just to prove that stressful story creation is a human condition from which none of us is immune.

As many of my followers know, I have four football-obsessed sons. As is so often the case, I was traveling the day that my younger boys played their city tournament game and I returned long after they had gone to bed. The next morning, I got up with the intention to be a fully present, caring mom to the boys in the few hours we would have together before I headed back to the airport.

The boys raced downstairs first thing, so excited. "Mom, we won the game! We won the whole tournament, we even beat the older kids!" Now, what would a fully present, kind, encouraging mother do when her boys give her that kind of news? I would hope that I'd congratulate them, tell them how proud I am of them, how great they are. I almost did, too, until the next words out of their mouths were, "And we have another game this morning—in an hour—and our uniforms are dirty!"

With that, my mind jumped to a story—the one about how I have to do everything around here and how their father is unsupportive and evidently incapable of planning ahead. So I skipped the praise and went straight to, "Where the heck is your dad?"

I found George upstairs, still in bed—lounging, it seemed to me—seemingly unconcerned. He even offered a potential solution. "Cy," he said, "no worries. I'll take the kids to the game early in their dirty uniforms, practice some tackling and rub 'em around in the field a bit and no one will ever know whether that dirt on their uniforms is new or old." I was horrified. What else went on here while I was gone? Did the kids get beer with breakfast? Blowing up my story that I had to do everything, that working women really do have a second shift, that stay-at-home moms would love to catch my brood arriving in dirty uniforms and judge me for it . . . I yelled at George, threw the uniforms in the washing machine, and got the kids to the game in the nick of time (uniforms slightly damp, but clean)—with everyone fully frustrated, distraught, and sad that our time together had been so stressful—just in time for me to head back to the airport.

On the way to the airport, I had time to mull over what had just occurred. I had acted based on my story rather than the facts: my kids told me they had won a championship and I yelled at them. George offered to help and I yelled at him. I spent my morning watching the laundry, wishing it would go faster, instead of enjoying time with the kids. I sent my kids out to play in wet uniforms as I contemplated divorce from their father, who is actually one of the most supportive partners around. George is willing to be the sole caregiver anytime I want or need to completely dedicate myself to the profession that I love. In fact, he was doing it right as I headed out of town! So you see, I'm also imperfect. When I got to the airport, I called home to apologize to everyone—for not giving them the benefit of the doubt, for not celebrating their success, and for jumping to conclusions. Once I confronted reality, I went very quickly from thinking that my family needed to change to seeing where I needed to change. The good news? I could rescue the situation by fixing what was wrong with my own mindset, dropping that self-inflicted drama.

In order to restore peace to your life, first you need to understand that the source of your suffering is not what happens to you but the stories you create about what happens to you. We all tell ourselves stories and live with the resulting drama, whether we are conscious of it or not. I call it "arguing with reality," and it's the single largest barrier to peace and success for most people. The only way to change it is by becoming aware of when and how you tend to do it.

Here are some other examples of what it sounds like:

"I shouldn't have to do this—it's not part of my job description."
"Other people should be more dedicated and motivated. Nothing would get done around here if it weren't for me."
"There's not enough time to get it all done."
"Our department is always having to clean up after others' mistakes."

"The boss just doesn't get it."

"He is always undermining me."

"My coworkers don't appreciate me."

"Management only cares about the bottom line."

"I'm underpaid for what I do here."

"It would be finished if they'd stop interrupting me with last-minute changes."

Learned Helplessness: Putting On the Shackles

You are arguing with reality whenever you judge your situation in terms of right or wrong instead of fearlessly confronting what *is*. When you are judging, you are not leading; not serving, not adding value. Your judgment is a waste of your time and energy—an opinion that cannot be proven and is only loosely based on the facts of a situation. When you argue with reality, you move away from the facts of a situation, assigning motive, making assumptions, and overwriting reality with a mental story, in which you are cast as the victim and someone else has all the power. On an average day, you and every other person in your organization waste two hours on unproductive thoughts like these. Over time, this habit of thought calcifies into a set of behaviors known as "learned helplessness,"[1] in which people begin to hold themselves back more effectively than any external circumstance or person ever could.

The perfect example of learned helplessness can be found at the circus. Have you ever wondered why the elephants—the strongest and largest animals in the circus—don't simply walk away? When an elephant is born, it only takes about two weeks for him to get strong enough to break his chains, but his trainers use this time to their advantage. The baby elephant, chained to a tree, will make many attempts to break free before giving up, but once he has given up, that's it. Although he grows

13

larger physically, in his mind, the chain is still stronger than he is. In effect, he imprisons himself. A lot of us live our lives the same way.

Learned helplessness is symbolized by battle fatigue, that moment when an issue is raised, people's eyes glaze over, and they say, "You know what? We've had that issue forever and there is really nothing we can do about it. We just have to learn to live with it." Humans may not be rational, but they are predictable. People will take a limitation from the external environment, internalize it, exaggerate it, and bolster it in their imaginations until they've shackled themselves. They tell themselves a story about what's possible and impossible, and that story informs their effort. Learned helplessness leads them to falsely attribute lackluster results to (fictional) wholehearted efforts.

For some time the conventional wisdom has been that we need to listen to unhappy employees, that leaders need to work on providing employees with the optimal circumstances in which to work. The conventional wisdom is wrong. If you encourage people to complain and to make excuses for their results, you encourage learned helplessness and the victim mentality that goes with it. You allow people to believe, in essence, "We cannot do our best work in suboptimal circumstances, and we are not 100 percent personally responsible for our results."

Personal Accountability in the Pursuit of Happiness

There is a competency that we have disregarded in the workplace for some time, and that is personal accountability. Personal accountability has great benefits for organizations, but it has an equal, if not greater, impact on the individual who practices it. (Pay attention, because I'm about to give you one of the best reasons of all to work on this.)

Those who study positive psychology used to think that happy people were ones who were not under stress. They have since discovered that happiness is not correlated with a lack of stress or a perfect environment.

(If it were, how many people could really describe themselves as happy?) It is correlated to the amount of accountability you accept in your life. That's right: the more responsibility you take for your results, the happier you will be. Which is really great news. Because seizing responsibility is a choice: to find peace and be happy and productive no matter what your circumstances. It has to come from inside. No one can give it to you, but no one can take it from you, either.

CY'S BOTTOM LINE	**Happiness is not correlated to perfect circumstances or a lack of stress in your life, but to the amount of personal accountability you accept.**

Once you realize this, it blows current theories of engagement out of the water. Leaders these days work so hard to keep employees happy—to keep them from being affected by the "shocks" of everyday working life. They hand out surveys and try to find out what they can do to reduce stress and perfect circumstances in the office. But in fact, none of this has any effect on employees' level of engagement. With the knowledge that accountability equals happiness, we can instead work to develop our employees so that they can have a real impact on what happens around them. Instead of trying to prevent the shocks (which is impossible anyway), we can help them become shock-proof.

If you are feeling deflated at the end of your day—or even sometimes at the beginning—I guarantee you that the stories you are telling yourself are like little holes in your tires letting all the air out. You will be happy and will have peace of mind to the exact degree that you accept responsibility for your results. Those who have learned this and other tools of Reality-Based Leadership leave the office energized, because they have had an impact and they have dealt with reality the entire day, to the best of their abilities.

At this point, you might be wondering what the appeal of arguing with reality and learned helplessness could possibly be. If this mindset is the root of all unhappiness, reduces productivity, increases drama, and poisons organizations, why does it persist? For one simple reason: it feels safer and easier to blame than to act. As long as we can blame something outside ourselves for our problems, we don't have to take responsibility for our actions. Often this is not a conscious thought. It manifests itself as frustration and poor results. If any of this sounds familiar to you, but you're still not sure of where your own organization stands in terms of drama, keep track of your answers to the following Yes/No questions.

Measuring Your Office's Freak-Out Factor

First, let's take a look at the behavior of the people in your office (since it's always easier to judge other people honestly than it is to judge ourselves):

1. Does your office suffer from Chronic Shock Syndrome (that is, are people in the habit of greeting change with surprise, panic, and blame)?
2. Are BMWs (bitching, moaning, and whining) common in your office parking lot?
3. Do people make decisions based on assumptions about the motivations of others?
4. When accounting for poor results, do people tend to use the words *they* or *me* or *us* with a lot of victim words (such as *ignored*, *screwed*, *excluded*) in between?
5. Do your coworkers spend more time judging and critiquing than they do helping one another?
6. Does feedback tend to be met with moping, defensiveness, or retaliation rather than change?
7. Are people more invested in being right than in getting the job done?
8. Do those around you exhibit signs of a victim mentality (lack of proactivity, "us versus them" attitude, believing themselves to be at the mercy of circumstances or fate)?

Next, how about your leadership?

9. Do you struggle with any of the following types of employees:

   a. Chronic underperformers

   b. Tenured employees whose skills are outdated

   c. Self-righteous top performers with an outsized sense of entitlement

10. Do you look around and see people who have mentally disengaged—but keep coming to work?

11. Do you look around and see people that you've mentally fired—but never told?

12. Do you still tolerate "That's not my job" as a response to a request?

13. Do you believe you are the only one in your organization who wants success as much as you do?

14. Do you spend most of your management time and energy on a few problem people while your best performers run on autopilot?

15. Do you and your employees spend more time playing not to lose than playing to win?

Count your "Yes" answers to assess your office's Freak-Out Factor.

1–5 "Yes" answers indicate a Distracting level of drama.

This level of drama will continue if you continue to allow it. It's time for you to step up as a leader. In Part Two, you'll learn Reality-Based coaching techniques that will help you get the most out of your people and reclaim time wasted on drama for productivity.

6–10 "Yes" answers indicate a Miserable level of drama.

You might as well put "drama" on your budget as a line item, because you are funding it in a big way. Chances are that much of the drama in your organization is starting with you. You'll need to start by working on yourself. In Chapters Two and Three, I help you get your mindset right. Then, you'll have to get relentless about changing the mindsets of your employees—or getting new employees. In the meantime, make this book your new best friend, or risk losing what you've worked so hard to build.

17

11–15 "Yes" answers indicate an Utterly Exhausting level of drama.

Time for a full-on cultural overhaul and Reality-Based Leadership intervention! It won't be easy, but it will be worth it when you see the results when your talent is used for productivity rather than drama. Drama will become a dirty word in your organization, and you'll see the effects in your bottom line. The turnaround starts now.

The best news in all of this is that through awareness comes change. Feeling bad about your level of drama won't improve the situation, but working with this book will. Drama is ultimately the result of a lack of clear leadership. If you as a leader do not embrace reality and deal with it directly, those you lead will not know how to invest the precious resources of their time and energy. That is why it's essential to start with you. Only when you have found the peace you need to lead will you be able to coach others effectively. In Chapter Two I show you a method that will help you begin to distinguish drama from fact and create new habits of thought: conscious and proactive ways to stop the argument with reality and start engaging fully with the world as you find it. It's the first and most important step to becoming a Reality-Based Leader.

2

If You Argue with Reality, You Lose (but Only 100 Percent of the Time)
How to Heal Your Relationship with Reality

Now that you recognize how destructive the habit of arguing with reality can be, and how little it serves you, it's time to let it go. This chapter centers on a very powerful idea: stress is not caused by what happens to us; it is caused by the stories we tell ourselves about what happens to us. Often these stories have no bearing on reality, and the truth is much less unpleasant than what we have imagined in our minds. I'm going to show you how to reduce your stress by questioning your stories and learning to tell different ones.

First, let's look at Figure 2.1 for the chain of events that leads from an event to its (albeit disappointing) results.

Event

Let's say you work in Order Fulfillment and you receive an order from the Sales Department. The order is missing information that would normally be gathered at the point of sale.

Figure 2.1

Missing information, in itself, is not so stressful. Think of how many birthdays and snail mail addresses are missing from your contacts list, for example. Maybe those are not big priorities—they're easy enough to get if you ever need them.

Thinking

Missing information has no emotion attached to it whatsoever until you start thinking—adding in your version of reality, your story, your judgment. Here is where the drama begins.

You might think, "Sales is so lazy. They make all the money and we do all the work. They don't care about the details or who they inconvenience. They probably did this on purpose because they know we always fix their mistakes. I am the only one committed to quality around here. Their manager should hold them to a higher standard. Now the order will be late and my department will be blamed. As usual." If you aren't upset enough already, you might dredge up anything else Sales has done in the past that showed their lack of respect for you and their ignorance of what it takes to deliver on their promises to customers.

Does it sound like I have been listening in on your conversations? I wish it were because I am so insightful, but unfortunately it's because there are no new stories. I have spent time in many companies, and drama looks the same in all of them. People repeat their stories so often, and so few leaders question them, that all involved begin to accept these stories as the truth.

Feeling

After you have created a story like this, you will begin to notice the feelings that follow directly from your mental work: stress, anger, fear, anxiety, righteousness, outrage, depression, low morale—to name a few possibilities. These feelings are what give rise to our actions.

Action

When you are feeling angry with Sales, disenfranchised from the organization, citing a profound lack of fairness, and needing to defend yourself from coworkers who are out to get you, you begin to act rude, shortsighted, defensive, and rule bound. Your creative problem-solving skills are not engaged and you are less than helpful, using your energy to complain, plan revenge, reject the order, or bounce it back with a request for an exhaustive level of detail to punish Sales—playing by the "rules" rather than doing whatever it takes to get the order through.

Results

If you follow any of the courses of action dictated by your feelings, your results will suffer. Orders will be delivered late, the Sales Department will feel unsupported, management energy will be spent developing procedures to force teamwork rather than focusing on long-term strategy. Customers will certainly not be impressed. This is the worst-case scenario that plays out countless times in countless organizations every week.

Many individuals decide on their own that they will respond to this painful series of events by disengaging. They decide, "If no one else cares, why should I?" They relinquish responsibility for their results,

21

exhibiting learned helplessness as described in Chapter One. Of course, this is no solution.

Others simply try to be professional, convincing themselves that even if they feel stressed, righteous, or angry at the failings of others, they won't let it show in their behavior. Have you ever worked with someone like that? Sooner or later, their resentment spills over or manifests itself in sarcasm, lack of helpfulness, tail-covering, and doing the bare minimum—or doing the right thing with the wrong attitude, which is almost as bad. This is not a formula for great results.

The one link in this chain that we tend to overlook is the only one that is within our control: our thinking. What if, instead of manufacturing a story, we just stuck with the facts of the situation—what we know for sure?

Respond to the Facts, Not to the Story

Any time something happens and your thoughts start to flow and you begin to feel that familiar tightness in your chest, interrupt the chain of events to ask yourself a few simple questions:

1. What do I believe in this moment?
2. What do I know for sure? (What are the facts?)

Go back to your story, to your assumptions, and inquire.

What do you believe in this moment? "Sales is so lazy." Do you know that for sure? Some of the evidence (in the form of a sale) doesn't support it. The truth is, it's impossible to know. What if they don't even know the information is missing? What if they forgot to ask for it? Perhaps they are lazy. Does it matter? In reality, all you know about this situation is that the Sales Department sold something, and you have an order that is missing some information.

What else are you believing in this moment? "The order will be late and our department will be blamed." Do you know that for sure? In reality, the order isn't late yet. But if the information isn't procured and filled in, it could be late, and Order Fulfillment will legitimately share in the blame for your contribution to that outcome.

This leads us to the next questions you should ask yourself, which are about how you choose to react based on your story.

3. Who am I as a manager or as an employee when I believe this story?
4. Without this story, what would I do to help?

If you react based on your story, that Sales is lazy and they do these things to spite you and your colleagues in Order Fulfillment, you might send the file directly back to Sales and refuse to fulfill it until they resubmit their completed request. That might make the order late and disappoint the customer. Who are you in that moment? If you put yourself in others' shoes, you have to admit that is self-righteous and downright tedious behavior, in which you're prioritizing being right and making a point over serving your customer. Do you want to be that person in your office?

What if, instead, you reacted based on the facts? What if you simply noted what information was missing, felt happy that you noticed it before it affected the customer, picked up the phone, and fixed the problem? You could simply call Sales, congratulate them on their sale, and ask a few more questions to get the missing information. Order fulfilled on time, your whole company looks like rock stars to your customer.

After you've eradicated your story in favor of embracing reality, all you are left with is a couple of extremely simple questions to answer:

5. How can I help?
6. What is the very next thing I can do to add value right now?

Try to answer these questions as specifically as you can, write down your answers, and consider them your Simple Instructions. Then, get busy following them. In this example, Sales is selling and you can add value by ensuring that the order is fulfilled correctly. After all, if Sales were perfect, why would the company even need you in Order Fulfillment?

The point of this exercise is to find out whether, and to what extent, you are responding to the facts of a situation versus your story (all of the thoughts you've made up about it). Our stories come from a deep, inner voice of doubt that we owe it to ourselves to question. These voices waste our time, they cause us to feel helpless, and they stop us from moving forward productively and getting the results we want. When the story is gone, all that remains are the two questions that lead directly to action. Answer them and move forward with conviction. Free your mind for innovation, problem solving, vision, creation, and improvement.

How you respond to a potentially stressful situation or person is up to you. Once you become practiced at asking yourself these questions, you will have developed the ability to step back, see things for what they are, skip the storytelling, and use your energy for impact. Once you commit to embrace reality, your choices will be much more conscious.

Watch for Three Common Stories

1. *Victim stories:* "It's not my fault." These stories make us out to be innocent sufferers.
2. *Villain stories:* "It's all your fault." These tales emphasize others' nasty qualities.
3. *Helpless stories:* "There's nothing else I can do." These stories convince us that we have no options for taking healthy action.

Professional Courtesy: Give Others the Benefit of the Doubt

There may be times when you still choose to believe a story instead of reality. I always advise my clients to practice professional courtesy. My definition of *professional courtesy* is to extend the benefit of the doubt to others—always. So, they're allowed to believe a story (that is, something they cannot absolutely know to be true) as long as they choose one that gives others the benefit of the doubt, preserves their accountability, and does not create more tension. This can be useful in motivating you to take that next right action and feel good about it instead of put-upon. For example, if you're the person in Order Fulfillment with the incomplete file, you can say to yourself, "Look! Sales must be so busy selling that they forgot to write this information on the customer's order. I'm glad it came to me because I'm great at noticing details and I can fix it without any interruption of service to the client." If this sounds like a parody of a good attitude to you, go ahead and roll your eyes, but making the call takes two minutes. Imagine how many of those calls we could make in the time most of us spend spinning out imaginary arguments with colleagues in other departments. In Part Two, I go deeper into how to coach other people in these techniques, but for now here's a quick tip from the trenches: When I can see that an employee, or a whole team of people, is upset and stressed, deep in their story, I refocus them with a couple of quick questions: "What do we know for sure?" and "How could we help?" When they have their answer about how they can help, I tell them to get busy and act on it.

We all have stories that hold us back. What's yours? Who would you be without it? How much time would you free up for other pursuits, and how much stress could you eradicate from your life? How wildly successful could you be? Next time you are faced with an event that starts your mind reeling, try this simple exercise my clients find extremely helpful.

New Story Exercise: Editing Your Story

Writing things down can help you tune in to your thoughts. It's especially useful when you are just beginning to use this method and listening to your thoughts is not yet automatic. Later on, continue to use it whenever you're so enmeshed in a situation that it's hard to step back and stop your mind from reeling. Whenever you are that stressed, take it as a sign that it's time to take a break, and do this exercise.

1. Sit down and write what is happening. This is not to share—it's just for you. So don't worry about complete sentences or paragraph structure, grammar or presentation. Just spew forth and write down exactly what you are thinking. Don't edit yourself or judge what you're writing. This could be a paragraph or it could be ten pages—it's whatever you need it to be, whatever you feel like getting out of your head and onto the page.

2. Get a highlighter, or just go through and underline every line that is stated as a fact.
   An example might be, "My boss does not support me."
   (If you still feel too close to the situation, take a break, take a walk around the block, listen to your iPod, pet your dog, or do some deep breathing before tackling the next step.)

3. Go through each of those "facts," and ask yourself, Do I know that for sure (that is, Is it really a fact or is it part of the story I am telling myself)?
   Maybe it is true that your boss is being unsupportive right now. Challenge yourself to come up with ways that the opposite could be true. If you can think of ways in which your boss is being unsupportive now, try to think of ways that she has supported you in the past.
   Separate the facts from your story as rigorously as if you were the editor of a newspaper. Edit out any judgment, anything you can't absolutely know to be true, anything that you couldn't prove with a source, any assumptions, any assignment of motive, and any premature conclusions.

4. On a separate page, write down the facts that have survived your rigorous questioning. You will be left with the things you absolutely know to be true. This is your reality. Everything else is your story.

5. Discard, shred, burn, or otherwise drop your story. Focus on the facts—your reality. Ask yourself what is the very next thing that you could do to add value and take the answer as your Simple Instructions. Then—follow through with action.

One of my clients, whom I'll call Karen, had an extraordinary breakthrough when she applied the tools from this chapter. Here's what happened.

Karen was an amazingly talented senior vice president in a financial company—in fact she was the first female SVP in the history of the company. She was very used to marshaling support for her ideas through presenting the information, showing how it was a "best practice" for organizations in current environments, and receiving the go-ahead from the powers that be.

For the first time in the history of her career, Karen had run into a group—her board—that hesitated to adopt Karen's recommendations after a thorough presentation. It seems that they weren't as swayed by the "We have to do this to remain in line with best practices" argument. In fact, following her presentation they proceeded to provide anecdotes from how they ran their own businesses (small businesses, not multibillion-dollar companies), they questioned whether or not it was even true that they had to go to so much effort to keep compensation aligned across the many positions (when in fact it is the law) and even questioned the pay of Karen, who seemed to be making a lot of money compared to most women they knew (bordering on justifying pay discrimination). Karen's idea was tabled and the board agreed not to put any more money behind these "new age" Human Resources ideas.

Karen was livid as she shared with me the blow-by-blow happenings at the board meeting—adding in many comments—some in parentheses accompanied by long diatribes about how "backward" and "behind the times" the board members were. She deemed them to be conservative male chauvinists who placed zero value on great talent. According to Karen, they were undeserving of their positions, were incapable of running the company, and were generally pretty despicable human beings.

As Karen took a look at her board—the one she would need to work with for the remainder of her career, upon whom she depended for approval for every single program she would like to implement—she became discouraged and began to talk about quitting the position she had worked for years to attain. She was outraged that she would have to leave when they were the ones with the shortcomings. At times she would decide to fight instead. After all, they were wrong; what they were doing could be deemed irresponsible and perhaps illegal!

I found myself in a coaching session with Karen a few days after this meeting, as she vacillated between flee and fight. I suggested that there might be another choice—a way of seeing the situation differently that would allow her to recognize the many opportunities at hand to learn great new ways of influencing, while being instrumental in bringing her board into the twenty-first century.

First, to help her get willing, we entertained the question, "If the universe is friendly, why would this be happening for your higher good?" Karen documented her answers, which were many but included:

- To best prepare for a CEO role someday, as CEOs have a responsibility to work with their boards and need to be masterful at managing those relationships
- To gain additional competency in influencing and persuading
- To learn more diverse ways of selling ideas and programs
- To increase her own confidence of her own value as she confronted familiar questions regarding her salary and worth as a resource
- To become more open to others' diverse views and to become more inclusive and more skilled at facilitating consensus

It seemed that this challenge was in fact brimming with opportunities to enhance Karen's competence. There seemed to be ample lessons at hand. I encouraged her by saying, "Let's get busy making sure you get every possible ounce of learning and development out of this experience."

Next, Karen documented what she was believing—her story of the board. She saw the board as closed-minded, conservative, incompetent, discriminating, incapable, backward, and from the Dark Ages. Next, she was able to see that when she believed this story, she tended to take a hard line—providing very few options, talking in terms of what the board "had to do," and threatening them with the legalistic take on consequences. She dramatically exaggerated the consequences, closed her mind to any ideas from the board that were different than her own, and showed her opinion of the board through her tone of voice and condescending attitude.

Karen was an old hand at the new story exercise and was quickly able to edit her story down to the simple facts. She had presented to the board. They had not been able to see clearly the value of her recommendations and had tabled the action until the next board meeting, stating they would like to learn more. Once Karen had edited her story, it became clear to her that her presentation had been fraught with shortcomings—especially when selling the idea. Her interpretation

28

of the board's intentions had been incorrect. Far from closed-minded, they wanted to learn more. They were willing to give her more time to revise her presentation and approach.

She was also amazed to see that what she believed affected her attitude and her behavior. It was even a bit painful for her to think of how unprofessional she had become in her relationship with the board.

Next, we entertained the fantasy of what type of SVP Karen would be in the presence of her board if she didn't have that story in hand. She would be open, she would be learning, she would be working to be of great service—in short, the kind of SVP they would find invaluable. She would have used her time to ask a ton of questions about what the board did value, what wasn't clear from her presentation, how she could help, what additional information they would like, and details from the board members' backgrounds and experiences that would help her better prepare for their next meeting. As it stood, unfortunately, she had very little additional information to guide her as she adapted her approach. She only had her inaccurate story portraying herself as a victim and the board as villains. She decided that she would rather be the SVP without the story.

This was such a great learning experience that we continued to use it to examine Karen's typical modus operandi and to see what else we could learn. She had described her board as closed-minded, conservative, incompetent, discriminating, incapable, backward, and from the Dark Ages. I asked her to think for a moment whether any member of the board could (possibly, hypothetically) ascribe those same attributes to her. Might any of them think that she had been closed-minded, conservative, incompetent, discriminating, incapable, backward, and from the Dark Ages? This part was painful—but breakthroughs always are.

Karen was amazed that she could find a lot of evidence to confirm that she herself had become quite closed-minded about the board. In fact, once she decided that she was right and that they were idiots, she quit trying to understand them. After all, what could they have to offer her (besides approval for her ideas . . .)? She could also see that she had proven incapable of convincing them of the value of her programs and even of her own value as a resource. She began to see herself as quite incompetent in working with a group that didn't grant instant adoration and approval. She had even discriminated against them, deciding that they didn't deserve to be granted any additional time or information due solely to their occupations, states of residence, and viewpoints that differed from her own. She had to admit to being in the Dark Ages—or at least in the dark—about what it was going to take to manage board relationships. She could see that she was backward, too, as she kept looking backward, wishing for the days when she was just a VP and didn't have to deal with "idiots" like this board.

What a great piece of inner work—the kind that changes your mindset and definitely changes the way you lead. Karen was able to free up her mind and her talent to get creative, to see the issue from all sides, and to better understand the board. From that very humble place (the one where she realized that she was capable of all that of which she had accused others), she was able to teach, persuade, understand, and ultimately craft a way forward, receiving board approval not of her plan but of the plan that they built together with her expertise and their input.

Your World Is a Projection of You

This exercise led Karen to radical acceptance of her role in creating her reality and completely changed her perspective. It can do the same for you. It is very rare that something happens to us that we do not co-create. Your world is a projection of you. What you give to others is what you get back most of the time.

Imagine you have gone to the grocery store and it is crowded. You are in a hurry. You rush around and maybe inadvertently push someone as you're trying to maneuver your cart around theirs. You have a scowl on your face because you have no time and you want what you want and you want it now. What is your experience of other people in that situation? You will encounter what you are projecting: rudeness, abruptness, selfishness. If, on the other hand, you take a few extra seconds to help someone; you say, "Excuse me," and "Thank you"; you smile at someone else in the checkout line. . . How does that change the experience people have of you and what they mirror back? On a very basic, subconscious level, that is co-creation, and it happens continually whether we are aware of it or not. I usually find that, when I have a belief, my mind tends only to collect those details that support it. So if I see someone as rude, and treat her rudely, when I get a rude response my mind is satisfied: "See? I was right!" It is a self-fulfilling prophecy.

Imagine you are walking down the hall in your office and you see a colleague. You say hello and she walks right by, doesn't say anything. You tell yourself, "She is so unfriendly. She thinks she is so much better than everyone else. Look, she is too important to even say hello! I can't stand stuck-up people." How are you going to respond to her next time you see her? You probably won't greet her. You won't offer her a doughnut before the meeting. You won't go out of your way to be friendly. And before long, whether or not her earlier failure to greet you was intentional, she will be mirroring your unfriendliness. You will have co-created the reality that you are not friendly to one another.

What have you got to lose by making that small extra effort to connect, by generously extending the benefit of the doubt? What if you walk past her, she doesn't return your greeting, and instead of telling yourself she is unfriendly, you think, "Wow—she's got a lot on her mind." Haven't you been there yourself? You're at the office eight or twelve hours a day and sometimes you go to that quiet place in your head where you are really mulling something over. You'd want your colleague to give you another chance, right? When someone fails to greet me, I choose to believe that her mind must have been elsewhere, she might not have even seen me. After all, everyone loves me—they just might not know it yet. Thank goodness I'm patient! (If you're going to give someone the benefit of the doubt, why not go whole hog?)

What if, on the other hand, the worst-case scenario is true? Your colleague is rude. She's out for herself and she doesn't care about you. She won't offer you a doughnut before the meeting and she isn't going to say hello in the hall. Even if all of that is true, what would be the most professional and civilized reaction? Why allow someone else to determine your behavior? The best course of action is still to make the effort. If I believe you are uncommunicative, I withhold communication. If I see you as hostile, I respond with hostility. It is all co-creation, so model the behavior you want to see.

31

Other people are rarely as focused on us as we are on ourselves. The rudest colleague in your office might be shocked to know how much you care about how he treats you, even as he might be obsessing over how someone else treats him. When our egos get involved, things always get messy. (More about that in Chapter Three.) For now, suffice it to say, it is natural for humans to be self-centered. Try not to get caught up in the need to prove your worth to people like that—it won't reflect well on you. You will usually get what you give, so give your best.

There are a couple more really great ways to look at this. One idea, which you saw Karen apply in the example, is that whatever you believe about someone else, you turn it around to check and see if it is actually more true of you. So, if I think that my colleague Sarah is always questioning me, I turn it around. After all, I am not Sarah. I cannot know for sure that she is always questioning me. Would it be more accurate to say, "I am always questioning Sarah"? Now, if there is some truth to that, then I can begin to understand that the issue is not so much about Sarah as it is about my own projections. I can stop questioning Sarah and trust that she has something to teach me.

A great mentor once told me, "Cy, whatever is missing in a situation is that which you are not giving. You go first." So, when I sat around the conference table with people who I was judging as closed-minded, she would ask me what was needed in that room. And I would say, "Open-mindedness." And she would say, "That is what you need to give." When I stopped judging and offered what was missing, it changed everything. I find this works almost every time, and the effect is immediate. Some might say that giving more when you feel a lack is a position of weakness. I would argue that it's actually a position of quiet strength. There's no capitulation or subjugation involved—just influence—and isn't that one of the strongest qualities a leader can exhibit? You can't force other people to give you what you think is missing, but if you can bring yourself to give it unconditionally, without manipulative intent, then you will find your generosity mirrored back to you.

| CY'S BOTTOM LINE | What is missing from a situation is that which you are not giving. |

Reality-Based Leaders are part of an inner peace movement. In this chapter, I have introduced methods that will help you bring a great sense of peace and acceptance to your work and your life. It might not happen overnight, but if you keep practicing it will happen. You'll get more of what you want and less of what you don't, and you'll let go of the stories that cause you stress. You'll get to a place where you believe that everyone you come into contact with is doing the best they can with what they've got. I believe that our true nature is to be kind and caring and helpful, and that anything that cuts off that energy, anything that separates us from another, is painful. If you want to end your pain, approach others with no story less generous than that. Cultivate a core belief that the universe is benevolent, and get busy working on the higher good.

Reality-Based Leaders simply refuse to argue with reality and so they never overreact. What you may notice as you question your stories is that the most stressful ones of all are the ones that place you in the center of the universe—the ones in which you are asking, in essence, "*Why* is this happening to *me*?" How can you make effective decisions, recognize and take advantage of opportunities, or inspire other people from a position of such weakness? And why would you want to?

Overreactions come straight from the ego, whereas the resolution to take the next right action comes from selflessness, from the desire to serve the greater good. The best leadership decisions are made from a place of equanimity and neutrality, when you keep an open mind, martial your energy, and accurately size up a situation before moving forward. Many of us don't realize how deeply attached we are to being right and to the approval of others. In Chapter Three, I show you how to begin to release yourself from that trap and find the true meaning of servant-leadership.

3

Would You Rather Be Right, or Wildly Successful?

There is a lot of big talk about leadership in the corporate world these days. Phrases like "engagement," "building trust," "succession planning," and "employee development" get bandied about. But from what I have seen, the amount of talk is inversely proportional to the leadership. Reality-Based Leaders are different. They are less talk, more action. They are willing to forgive, to refrain from judging others, and to serve. Reality-Based Leadership is humility in action, and humility requires that you give your ego a rest. Everyone has heard of the ego, and you might even think that a little ego is healthy, necessary, even, to lead others and succeed.

Ego: Not to Be Confused with Confidence

There is a difference between being confident and being ego-centric. Confidence—having faith in your abilities—is an essential quality in a leader. I would go so far as to say that no great leader is without it.

35

Ego is something else entirely. It serves as the organized, conscious mediator between you and your reality, affecting your perception of and adaptation to reality. When a person's actions are motivated mostly by his own wants or needs, when someone seems incapable of comprehending anyone else's perspective, we say that person is ego-centric. In general, confidence moves you forward; ego holds you back. They are quite distinct, and they are not always correlated.

The ego's job is to seek approval, accolades, appreciation, and validation at all costs. And it can be a high price to pay, both in terms of relationships and results. Ego-centric behavior keeps you from serving your clients and your organization, and it makes you emotionally expensive to your employer. Why? The ego loves drama, whether it's the drama of collusion when colleagues gather in the break room to complain (I call this "the meeting after the meeting") or the drama of having to go it alone on a team effort because you are convinced that no one else cares quite as much or can get the job done quite as well as you can. It is one thing to work hard out of a sense of dedication, commitment, and love for your work. It is another thing entirely to be a self-righteous martyr who resents and judges others. If you live to compare, and other people are always coming up short in your estimation, chances are, it's all about you.

CY'S BOTTOM LINE	A bad day for the ego is a good day for the soul of a leader.

Ego Motivation Masquerading as Selflessness

Sometimes, ego-centrism is easy to spot in yourself. You might have felt an uncomfortable sense of recognition on reading the previous paragraphs. (If so, read on because we get to rehab recommendations shortly.) One rule of thumb is that if you often worry about coming across as ego-centric, you probably aren't; whereas if it has never occurred to you, then you might be. Sometimes, it's not so straightforward, and it's easy to delude yourself about this. Ego motivation is at its most insidious when it masquerades as selflessness. Here are some of the warning signs:

- Are you excessively worried about offending others in the course of doing your job and concerned that they will not like you?
- When you have been empowered to make a decision, do you find yourself consensus building long after you have the information you need—instead of simply making the decision?
- Do you avoid confrontation and potential conflict to the point of making extra work for yourself or others (for example, pussyfooting around people who might be affected by a decision you make, or withholding unpopular yet essential information until the last possible moment)?
- Do you often have resentful thoughts such as "This place would fall apart without me" or "People have no respect for what my job entails"?

Does any of this sound familiar? When your goal, above all, is to be seen as right, to be loved and approved of at work, like it or not, that means you are operating from personal motives, for personal rewards. That makes you emotionally expensive to your employer. Your productivity is likely suffering because you put too much of your effort into proving that you are right and deserve to be valued and appreciated. If you want to be truly valuable to your employer, check your ego at the door!

Ironically, one of the personality types that most often falls into this trap is the people pleaser who has trouble saying, "No." People pleasers tell themselves that they are fundamentally generous and self-sacrificing, when they are spending half of their working hours spinning their wheels on extra projects they have willingly taken on—let's face it, for ego gratification—at the expense of their real jobs.

People pleasers are prime targets for another type of ego-centric, the one who will take advantage by dumping unwanted work on them, knowing that "What would I do without you?" is a bigger turn-on for a pleaser than booze or pills. These divas will return just in time for the curtain call, stealing all the limelight if things go well, but they'll be the first to duck backstage when the tomatoes start flying.

Then there are the consensus builders. To a degree, consensus building is constructive . . . until the moment when it isn't. How to tell? If you are stalling on a decision, trying to find a way to move forward without stepping on anyone's toes, then you are letting your fear of being disliked stop you from doing your job. You're creating extra work for yourself and the people who work for you. Any decision you make is going to upset someone. Far better to forge ahead with a decision that reflects a goal larger than yourself or your colleagues, so that when the disgruntled come to you to complain, you can be confident that it's not about you and it's not about them, either.

Table 3.1 Organizational Goals Versus Motives: How to Tell the Difference

Goals	Motives
Learn.	Be right/loved.
Find the truth.	Save face/look good.
Produce results.	Keep the peace/avoid conflict.
Strengthen relationships.	Punish/blame.

Work to Be Successful Rather Than Right

If some of these ego-centric behaviors are currently part of your repertoire, you can recover. It's up to you whether your actions fuel drama or results.

Depersonalize Your Work Environment

You have definitely personalized your work when you are spending your precious time and energy trying to get others to believe that you are right, that they were wrong, or that you should be appreciated more than you are. If you forgo the need for credit and focus solely on what you can do next that will add the most value, you will be accomplishing organizational goals and you will be emotionally inexpensive (that is, drama-free) for your organization. This is not to say you should not have friends at work, or that it's bad if your colleagues like you. What I am saying is, keep it professional and be liked for the right reasons. Get respect for your results. If you consensus-build to the point of paralysis, you won't make the tough, timely decisions that leaders have to make. If you treat your office like a popularity contest, you'll play it safe and sacrifice results. If someone complains about one of your tough decisions—and someone always will—then guess what? That is not your problem. You have acted as a professional in the service of a higher goal. In that situation, the complainer is the one being unprofessional. But—and this is a big *but*—the minute you point that out to anyone (with the possible exceptions of your mother, your spouse, and your best friend), you forfeit the high ground. That leads us to the next step.

Rid Yourself of Defense

Know that defense is the first act of war. Any response more energy intensive than "Good to know" is a declaration of war against reality, and you risk missing an opportunity in the situation. If you find yourself at war, immediately stop defending. Instead of voicing your first reaction, use phrases like, "Wow," "Good to know," "I see," "Thanks for sharing," and "Here's how I can help." Find a place of neutrality, where you are not attached to any prerequisite, circumstance, or outcome. It is from that neutral place that the best leadership decisions are made. You'll

39

know you are ready to lead when you can greet every change and surprise with "Good to know. Thank you." Followed by "This is a great opportunity—let's get started."

Aim for Common Ground, Not Knee-Jerk Criticism

If you feel violated by a goal or a decision made by someone else, here is what I suggest: Consciously agree with the person, immediately and without reservation. This is a tool I borrowed from improv comedy. In improv, actors have to make up and act out a scene, on the spot, without any pause for consultation. One starts talking, the other responds, and it all unfolds spontaneously from there. Improv is hard for a lot of reasons, not the least of which is that we all want to feel in control. But the first rule of improv is surrender. You must respond to every assertion from your colleague with "Yes, and . . . ," never "No, but . . ." After all, if one actor said, "We're at the zoo," and another said, "No, we're on the moon," the audience would be lost. You don't go against what your confederate says; you play along and build from there. Otherwise, the whole scene falls apart.

So, when someone at your office makes a goal or a decision that you want to reject because it's not the one you'd have made (assuming the person is being ethical), aim for common ground instead of knee-jerk criticism. Size up a new situation quickly and ask yourself, "What is the next right action I could take that would add value?" If you aren't sure, ask, "What can I do to help?" and then follow the Simple Instructions.

Many bright and talented professionals derail themselves by editorializing, critiquing decisions, and even withholding their expertise in order to prove a point. What begins as letting off a little steam or even chiming in with one's opinion can quickly turn into a habit that, over time, leads others to question your buy-in, alignment, and willingness to do whatever it takes to ensure success. Resistance squanders a great deal of energy that could be used to validate and contribute to the effort rather than attempting to block it or redirect it in a self-serving way.

Work to be successful rather than right. If you anticipate potential risks in a colleague's plan, work constructively on mitigation instead of nitpicking. (More on that in Part Two.) If you still can't get to that happy place, keep in mind that those who give their support freely are not only secure in their current jobs but are also extremely marketable to hiring organizations. Search for the opportunity in your challenges. Ask yourself, "If the universe is at least benevolent [as was concluded by Einstein], what are at least three reasons that what is happening is happening for the higher good?" Invest your energy and talent to bring these opportunities to fruition. Make your list of what you can do to add value, and get busy making that happen.

When Things Go Wrong . . .

If and when things go wrong, whether the fault lies with you or someone else does not matter. Instead of casting blame, or digging in your heels and justifying why it was right to do exactly as you did, drive for results or learning. Begin accounting, openly and honestly, for how you got your current results. You will move quickly from being a victim of circumstance to a professional who can account for the many actions and thoughts that led to the setback. You will either learn something that will help you get better results next time or you will find a way to improve the situation. Ask yourself, "Would I rather be right, or wildly successful?" If your choice is that you would rather be right, know that you will be giving up the potential for good results and valuable knowledge for the privilege of being right. That is because, when you decide that you are right, you immediately become righteous and close your mind against any external feedback to the contrary.

Being right, just for the sake of being right, is not worth what it costs you. Companies that are thriving in challenging times are happy, flexible, and profitable. They are fun places to work. Companies where people are hyperfocused on being right are very miserable places to work.

I worked with a pretty effective leader named Steve who oversaw the activities of five departments. The very first time we met, he shared with me that he was doing great with four of his five departments but really needed my help with the product team. While I truly believe that every one of us has something we need to develop next, I prefer to work on the person in front of me, so I asked him about the product team to see if a change in his mindset might be the first step in finding a productive way forward.

Steve shared with me that the product team was filled with super-negative people—most of whom were older and had been with the company for a long time. He was convinced that they resented him being their boss, as he was from the outside and much younger. While I am very comfortable with providing feedback to help people sign up or sign out of the company, a leader is not ready to give that feedback while he is still judging. When you are judging, you are not leading.

I asked him what their interactions were like. He gave me many examples. He dreaded their calls, and he usually let them go to voicemail first so he could take his time crafting his response and decisions. He met with them as seldom as possible, as the meetings were painful and filled with long lists of unaddressed issues and requests they made. He made sure that he always scheduled a meeting directly following his meetings with the product team, and let them know up front that he only had one hour for them, nothing more. He tended to space out when they tried to make him understand how things used to work, which was much more efficient according to them—after all, he had heard it all before.

At this point I started to laugh out loud. Steve, a bit offended, practically demanded that I tell him what was so funny. I was seeing life from the product team's perspective. I have a boss who avoids contact with me, lets my calls go to voicemail, responds to me only after extensive thought about his defense strategy, spaces out during our meetings, and cuts the meetings short. I asked Steve, "Are they always negative, is that true? When you ask them about their grandkids, do they light up?" It may not be factual to say that they are *always* negative. But it does seem they are consistently negative about Steve.

Now, I am not condoning the product team's behavior, but I am working with Steve, and the first place we can all start is where we are. Steve knows he needs help changing how he manages the product team, but his biggest obstacle is his belief that they are a negative group. What if he just dropped that whole story and simply responded to reality directly? The phone rings? Answer it. The team asks a question? Answer it, or teach them where to find the answer. The team shares what worked in the past? Listen and lead them into the future. The team requests some time with their leader? Engage with them—lead!

When Steve began to lead the team rather than judge and criticize, the team began to change for the better. Steve gained some respect and a platform on which to build the team through feedback and individual development of its members. When he quit minimizing, the team quit exaggerating. When he quit ignoring, the team quit screaming for attention. When he engaged, the team got clear about expectations— what they needed to do, and with what attitude—in order to be successful. And they had a role model of what positive, engaged behavior looked like—rather than the negative, disengaged example Steve had given them in the past.

When you focus your energy on what you are able to give and create rather than what you receive, you are truly serving. A contribution freely given, above and beyond who's right and wrong, whose job it is, who screwed it up, and whether or not it is supposed to be like this, is one of amazing value without the emotional drain and drama.

But beware that unnecessary drama can also result from avoiding confrontation when there's a legitimate need to resolve a situation or clear the air. If you need to give someone negative feedback, if you need to let someone go, if you need to ask someone for help—do not wait. It always takes less energy to have a legitimate confrontation than it does to keep avoiding it. Confronting doesn't create half as much drama and tension as holding back. You have nothing to fear if you are working in the best interests of your organization and remain professional and kind regardless of the reaction you get in return.

Learn and Grow from Feedback, Especially If It's Negative

Sooner or later, practically all of us receive negative feedback, whether it's in the form of poor results, a talking-to from the boss, or a colleague who cares enough to be honest. It can be hard to take, even when you know you deserve it or the bearer of the news is doing you a favor. So, what do you do when the voices of doubt are coming at you from outside? Here are five steps to gleaning the maximum benefit from negative feedback. Bad feedback does not have the power to stall your career, but an unwillingness or inability to absorb it and act on it does. Don't avoid the teachers in your workplace. Treat them as valued coaches who show you what you need to work on. Your coach will not necessarily come to you with the attitude of a cheerleader.

1. The first step is to welcome the news. This message has come to you as a sign of the next thing you need to work on to be successful. Even if you disagree at first, commit to the possibility that the messenger might be right. Respect and gratitude should be your default setting.

2. Check your ego and see what you can learn. The ability to receive feedback from the market, a client, our coworkers, or any other source without defensiveness or reaction is key for Reality-Based Leaders. Reactions come from our egos; right action comes from our commitment to work toward a goal greater than ourselves. Always respond to feedback with openness and a willingness to change.

3. If you struggle to take in the message, try this exercise one of my mentors gave me when I was very young and hated getting feedback. (It will stop you from doing what I used to do, which was to personalize it and get defensive and angry.) She gave me five options, and when I got feedback, I could only react by choosing one:

    a. "Thank you for caring enough about me to give me that feedback."

b. "I've noticed that about myself too, and it's something I'm working on."

c. "Will you help me to improve?"

d. "I am willing to see if I can find some truth in that."

e. "I used to think that about myself, too, and here is what I did to change it."

When somebody says something to me that is surprising, and I need to center myself, (d) is my favorite option. But any of these reactions will neutralize your defenses and give you a chance to go away and think things through before responding further. If you can admit to the fact that, as a human being, you are imperfect and you are still developing, it shows thoughtfulness and humility.

4. If you have the urge to ignore negative feedback, or quit, first ask yourself if the universe is trying to tell you something! When faced with a situation that has the potential to be our greatest teacher, the first thing we usually think about is how we can extricate ourselves from it. That's a normal, human reaction. But if you stay, and wholeheartedly confront the message you have been given, you move from being a victim of your circumstances to a professional who can account for the actions and thoughts that led to her results. You will come away from this experience stronger than before. If you decide you're unwilling to learn and grow and address the situation, and you walk away, know that what you don't welcome and address head-on in your life will reappear again until you get the intended lesson.

Are you willing to do whatever it takes to learn and grow from negative feedback? If so, on to the fifth step.

5. Stay in your lane, and you will be on the fast track to recovery. Focus on yourself—your development, your assumptions, your choices, and the actions you can take to regain your credibility and improve. Resist the urge to point out how others were involved in the poor outcome. It will only slow your progress and compound the negativity. Turn this into a positive experience by focusing only on what you can affect—your own thoughts and behavior.

The most important integrity gut check comes in the form of a simple question: "Can those around me identify my organization's goals from watching my behavior?" If not, change your behavior in support of the goals. Personally, I try every day to let go of the need for love, approval, and appreciation, because when I operate from those motives, my behavior deteriorates quickly. If, instead of focusing on what I can get, I focus on what I can give, I am always happier and more energetic. At the end of the day, I feel better. When you act in the best interests of your organization and enjoy the results of your effort, you lose your appetite for approval. You are free to act without fear, sugarcoating, or tiptoeing around others, resulting in higher productivity, more respect, and less stress all around. That is the mark of a true Reality-Based Leader.

ADDITIONAL RESOURCES: THE ALIGNMENT SURVEY

Before you move on to Part Two, turn to Appendix 1 and take a look at a survey that will show you what you are up against as you prepare to try a new method of coaching.

Restore Sanity to the Workplace

Once you have let go of your suffering, arguments with reality, and ego motivation, you will have a lot more time and energy to lead others: to help them find the freedom you have found and to achieve the goals you set as a company. In Part One, you learned methods to restore peace for yourself. Now it's time to share it with your team and call them to greatness. You'll learn more about a style of coaching that inspires and encourages everyone to take a Reality-Based approach to their work. It starts with differentiating between managing and leading. That is the focus of Part Two.

4

Lead First, Manage Second

If you have been promoted to a position of leadership in your company, chances are you have long since proven yourself as a manager. You're a whiz at solving problems, deciphering the spreadsheets, and balancing the budget. You know where to go to get the resources you need and how to ask for them in a way that gets the order signed. These are all critical competencies, but they do not prepare you to lead. In fact, they can get in the way of your becoming a Reality-Based Leader.

This idea is counterintuitive—even irritating—to some people the first time they hear it. Some of the executives I coach have never considered that there is a difference between managing and leading, much less that there are certain kinds of work that you have to delegate to become a great leader. I have had many clients expound on the philosophy that no task should be beneath anyone in their organization—that the leader should not ask anyone else to do that which he is unwilling or unable to do himself. I couldn't agree more; as a leader, you shouldn't delegate believing anything is "beneath" you. But you do need to set priorities and determine the best use of your talents and your company's resources.

Much of the insanity that takes place in most workplaces every day is due to a lack of leadership, plain and simple. Too many leaders hide behind their proficiency at logistics and dealing with complexity—the small picture—and hope that somehow the overall vision—the big picture—will fall into place. But I promise you, this is not going to happen by accident. You have to put down the spreadsheet and learn to lead first, manage second.

The difference between management and leadership is that management is working on your business, and leadership is working on your people. Leadership is about winning hearts and minds and consistently calling employees up to greatness by insisting on—and investing in—their growth and development. Leadership is working on the overall willingness, morale, and capacities of employees rather than micromanaging and becoming overinvolved in their daily activities. If you've ever watched five-year-olds play soccer, the "huddle ball" effect is very similar on a team in which the leader is over-managing and under-leading: too many players out of their zones, all trying to bring the ball up the field at the expense of the ultimate goal.

Over-Managing and Under-Leading

How exactly might over-managing and under-leading manifest in your office? Think back to the last time your organization went through a change and you needed everyone to pull together. When people learned about the change, did they race off to their desks, and look industrious for a while, only to return to you with a laundry list of the extras—time, money, people, and other resources—they needed in order to make it happen? If so, they see you as a manager, not a leader.

Do you get interrupted every 20 minutes throughout your day with questions that employees could answer themselves with a little bit of effort? If you drop everything and answer them . . . you are managing, not leading.

Have you ever had to put an important client on the back burner to deal with an in-house crisis? If so, you are definitely still managing, not leading.

Are you able to go on vacation without fielding "emergency" calls from the office? If not, bad sign. (On some level, though, doesn't it make you feel good to be needed? If so, that's an even worse sign!)

All of these are situations in which people come to you with problems they expect you to solve for them. Often, in difficult times, our first impulse is to try to perfect people's circumstances by providing resources, answers, solutions, or just our reassuring presence. We often try to manage our way out of difficulties—which effectively leaves our people behind—when we should be leading the way out in such a way that they feel supported, involved, and have the opportunity to learn from their challenges.

I'll let you in on a secret all Reality-Based Leaders know: The more you provide, the more people will need, and the less satisfied they will be with what you offer. It may feel good to play the benevolent boss or indispensable colleague, but trying to perfect people's circumstances is not the way to do it, because people gain nothing from being managed in that way. You risk robbing them of their sense of engagement and personal responsibility (which is also the source of all motivation and happiness). Your competence, which has gotten you so far, will become their excuse not to progress. You can—and should—learn other ways of being benevolent and indispensable.

A leader's primary job is to manage resources, and it is highly likely that the only resource in your budget with unused or untapped potential—indeed the only upside to be had in most businesses today—is the talent and energy of your employees. Reality-Based

51

Leaders continually work to make use of every bit of that potential, helping people to harness the energy they would normally expend on drama and redirect it toward activities that have the greatest possible positive impact in the organization.

"Problems cannot be solved by the same level of thinking that created them."
—ALBERT EINSTEIN

Reality-Based Leaders help people to change their mindsets, knowing that beliefs—not circumstances—are the greatest predictor of results. Offer people a compelling purpose and a new perspective instead of easy answers. If you habitually interrupt the patterns of thought that are holding people back, they will ultimately learn to solve their own problems autonomously and to succeed in spite of their circumstances. That is the mark of a healthy individual and a healthy organization.

Six Principles for Leading First, Managing Second

When working with clients, I have identified six principles that help them learn to lead first and manage second. Each is aligned with a coaching technique that engages people and develops their sense of personal responsibility and independence. I explain the principles and the coaching techniques, and then, near the end of the chapter, I introduce a groundbreaking new approach to employee surveys. My method allows you to create a culture of accountability by rewarding your top performers, giving more weight to their suggestions than you do to those with a mindset of resistance or learned helplessness.

Before you begin to apply these principles, a word of caution: In order for any of these techniques to work, those you lead must first be convinced that you truly care about them. It is your demonstrated respect and commitment that will allow them to trust you to help them reach their full potential.

Principle 1: Resist the Urge to Add More Value

You may already have suspected that the first principle would be about giving less and expecting more. If your people are used to being managed by you, instead of being led, don't be surprised if at first they feel you are being ungenerous. Persist, and they will come to appreciate your belief in their abilities. Reality-Based Leaders know that high expectations are a gift, and that it is not generous or loving to give someone that which they are capable of providing for themselves. It sends a message that you lack confidence in them. We need to adopt the "fall-back" position of confidence in others' abilities. The way to build confidence in people is to first show our confidence in their talent and critical thinking and to engage them in clear and direct discussions about what they can do. A theme of Reality-Based Leadership is *You go first*. You as a leader have to take the lead.

If every time employees come to you to complain about a situation, you commiserate, jump in to help, or go to your boss to request extra resources for them, you are only reinforcing their belief that you are there to perfect—or protect them from—their circumstances.

If someone comes to you in a state of learned helplessness, seeing only lack and impossibility, the best action you can take is to interrupt her thinking and help her get to the bottom of her "story." It all goes back to what you learned in Chapters One and Two: our mindsets and the stories we tell ourselves are the sources of most of our suffering, and any stressful thought we have is most likely untrue. Share the tools from Part One that have worked for you, especially the two questions that bring you back to reality every time: "What do we know for sure?" and "What can you do to help?"

Note that this advice is different from the advice I gave you in Part One—to pitch in wherever you see the opportunity, instead of keeping score. The difference is one of roles. When you are working with your peers, what is most valuable is action. But when you are someone's leader, you have a higher responsibility to help that person develop. You must use your judgment, based on the role you are fulfilling in the moment, whether your best course of action is to help or to coach.

You might be thinking that it's a lot quicker just to answer the employee's question or solve her problem, so you can move on to more important things. If this were a one-time interruption, you'd be right. But the deeper problem that led her to your door, and that keeps her dependent on you, will remain until you address it. It is less time consuming, in the long run, to invest in coaching. Essentially, you are teaching her to change her mindset and behavior in the way you learned to do in Part One.

The technique of reframing can dislodge your most habitual doorway hoverers. Reframing is helping people to see their circumstances differently so that they can have an impact on reality and understand their roles in co-creation. I like to tell people: Pray not to change your circumstances but instead to see your circumstances differently. Every challenge contains an opportunity. What you see really is what you get.

When someone comes to you in a state of panic, instead of mirroring that, or adding her problem to your own to-do list, remain calm and draw out her story. You will recognize it when you hear it, because there are no new stories.

Let's go back to the same example from Part One: "The other department left information out of the fulfillment request they sent us, and now the order will be late, and our department will be blamed."

That is problem and story in one neat package: the problem (missing information), and the story (late order, blame), the victim (our department), the aggressor (them).

Coach the person to separate the stressful story from the plain fact that the information is missing, so that it becomes a matter of taking responsibility for finding the missing information. Lead her back a step in her logic by asking some questions:

"Why do you assume the order will be late?"

"Isn't it lucky that you have noticed the missing information in time to prevent that happening?"

"What would you want the other team to do if they figured out an error on our part?"

"Do you have a plan for what you'll do next?"

Reframing the situation from one in which she is a victim to one in which she is in control will lead her to her own best solution.

If it is not immediately clear what the person's story is, it could be there is a genuine crisis, or she is trying to cover her tail because she knows she has contributed to a crisis that may erupt in the near future. That could go something like this: "The client is really angry because the order is late, but it's not my fault." Or, "The client may be calling you if the order is late, but I did everything I could with the information I was given by the other department."

If you get one of these, lead the person to take responsibility for her role in co-creation of the results. Help her to account for the ways in which she is contributing to the situation. What did she choose, deny, assume? Where did she fail to act? (Sometimes, failure to act is an action.) Did any of her actions hurt rather than help? If you validate her victim mentality, it will keep her dependent, whereas if you talk to her about ways she could have prevented the scenario from unfolding, you encourage her to think proactively in the future. The question she should be asking is not, "Whose fault is it?" but "Regardless of what went before, what is the next right action I can take to improve the situation?"

Finally, you may be tempted to take this angry client right off her plate and add him to yours. If at all possible, coach the employee to go back and rectify the situation herself, by calling the client back and apologizing, and making amends, whether it's by rushing the order, offering a discount, or another incentive to give your company a second chance. What works extremely well with service recovery is to admit the ways in which we disappointed the customer and ask how we can make it right by them. Your coaching session should provide a great rehearsal for that conversation.

When people come to you in a challenging situation, your job is not to tell them the opportunity they are not seeing. That just leads to greater frustration and defensiveness. Instead, help them to inquire on their mindsets. Find out how they are reading the situation. Be their student instead of the other way around.

The point of reframing is to help people get to a visionary mindset, in which they see themselves as the authors of their solutions, and take responsibility, instead of coming to you every time. Once they internalize that your response will not be to take the ball and run with it but to bounce it right back to them, they will start looking for ways to handle things on their own.

Principle 2: Coach the Person in Front of You

How often do people come into your office in blaming mode? You can tell just by the way they phrase their questions, always with reference to something—or someone—other than themselves. People persist in coming to you because they see you as a referee or as someone who will collude and commiserate with them. Either way, it's a time-sink for you both. If you let these complaints hook you, before you know it you will be involved in a fruitless, energy-draining conversation about the motives and actions of a third party who is not even in the room with you.

Early in my career, when I was leading a clinic operations group in health care, I had a wonderful top performer named Susan. Susan was detail oriented, committed to the organization, a fast learner, a true go-getter, and (most of the time) a team player.

She appeared at my door one day wanting to talk about a new coworker named Tammy. She was very upset by the fact that Tammy had been late four times in the previous week but had lied on her timesheet, stating that she was on time each morning.

If I had been over-managing and under-leading, my temptation would have been to overlook the person in front of me—the opportunity presenting itself at this moment—and launch an investigation into the dishonesty of the newest member of the team. And while that temptation would have been justified, it would have done nothing to move my team forward.

Thankfully, I had been coached to lead first and manage second—to work with the person in front of me. So I sought first to interrupt Susan's thinking by responding to her distress about her coworker by asking, "You had a coworker late four times this week? What did you do to help her?" Somewhat shocked by my refocusing question, Susan responded, "I did nothing to help her. I just judged her and am here tattling on her." And with that, she began to chuckle with self-awareness.

I asked her if she was in the mood to learn how she could improve. She agreed, so I began to ask a lot of questions, starting with how she had originally become aware of the problem, and her story quickly took shape. A coworker who was also late noticed that Tammy had written in the wrong time on her card and felt angry. She may have been late, too, but at least she was honest about it! She visited Susan and spent 30 minutes or so filling her in on the matter. Together, they enlisted the help of one more of my top performers and set up a stakeout. In the morning they would all keep an eye out for Tammy and document the time she arrived. Later, they would meet in the break room and compare the time on Tammy's card with the time they had actually seen her come in. The three of them had even kept a spreadsheet on the running total difference. They focused on Tammy for the first half-hour each morning and gossiped about her periodically throughout the day, presumably while neglecting their own duties.

As I inquired on Susan's focus and reviewed her spreadsheet on Tammy, I began to add up the cost to the company of Tammy's crime versus the cost to the company of Susan and her accomplices' focus on it. Tammy had potentially stolen about $60 from the company, given her hourly wage and benefits (about 30 minutes per day, four days a week at $10 per hour), but Susan and her two coworkers had spent about 2 hours per day watching for Tammy, talking about Tammy, and tracking her indiscretions. I totaled their time—at top salaries, plus the opportunity cost of what they could have accomplished in the time they allocated to Tammy. The total? $1,700!

Susan was astounded when I explained my math and showed her the totals, asking which was the bigger crime. Now, I was not justifying Tammy's behavior, and I would certainly address the issue with her, but what impact could Susan have had if she had chosen to help rather than judge? Judging is expensive and it has huge consequences. If I had ignored Susan and begun the witch hunt on Tammy, I would have wasted the opportunity to coach Susan on a potentially life-changing lesson: To be self-righteous and judgmental is never the best approach. The minute you become righteous, you are no longer a top performer. In fact, your crime could be bigger than the person's you are judging.

Imagine a workplace in which, when someone is late, instead of jumping to conclusions, colleagues jump in to help. They call to make sure the person is all right, offer to help, cover the phones, and greet her with a welcoming attitude, "I know you hate being late so we got you all set up and have your coffee waiting. Hope it helps your day go better!" What a difference that effort would make. If you were that person, and you were capable of signing up, you would—because that team rocks! If you were a chronic underperformer, however, you would stick out like a sore thumb and you wouldn't even be able to use the favorite excuse of poor performers, which is, "My teammates are mean to me, judge me, make it uncomfortable to be here, to ask for help..." An underperformer would probably opt out of this team fairly quickly, making room for another top performer who would fit in better.

The Christmas following our coaching session, I received an amazing gift from Susan—a book recounting a story told by a Buddhist monk. Two monks, one older and one very young, were walking to town for supplies when they came across an elderly woman struggling to cross a muddy, deeply rutted road. One of the clearest instructions in their vows had been that they must avoid contact with members of the opposite sex. Without a moment's hesitation, the older monk went to the woman, picked her up, and carried her across the road. The younger monk was flabbergasted, yet said nothing as they walked on. Four hours later, when he could not stand it any longer, he confronted the older monk. "What were you thinking, violating your vows so flagrantly, without any remorse? You touched a woman, you carried her all the way across that street." The older monk smiled and replied, "Interesting, I carried her for two minutes, in the spirit of helping. You have carried her for four hours, in the spirit of judging... if only in your mind. Whose vows are more violated?"

I was on cloud nine. Susan had gotten the message loud and clear and become an even more productive member of the team by focusing her energies on helping, not judging. A leadership victory. That is why you should focus on the person in front of you.

If you teach people to redirect their energy from collusion, assigning blame, and planning defensive moves, they can spend their time more creatively and productively. An added benefit? Once it becomes clear that you will always focus on the person in front of you, you should get many fewer visits from the busybody patrol.

Principle 3: Work on Confidence First, and Competence Will Follow

Another way you can foster independence is by asking twice as many questions as you answer. When you answer a question with a question—provided it's the right kind of question—it's an opportunity to build people's confidence.

Back when I was working as a coordinator for doctors' office managers, I was responsible for anywhere from eleven to twenty managers at a time. I also happened to be an expert at DSM (*Diagnostic and Statistical Manual*) coding, which is vital to maximizing reimbursement from Medicare and other sources. All day long, people would come to me and ask, "How do we code [fill in the blank] procedure to make sure we get reimbursed by [fill in the blank] insurer?" It got very repetitive.

At first, I would tell them the code, write up a policy, put it in a memo, and distribute it to everyone—with the result that no one else ever took responsibility for coding decisions. But soon I realized that I was actually failing my managers by making these judgment calls for them. DSM coding is not a simple matter of looking up numbers in a book; it is a complex system about which they needed to be confident.

59

The only way for them to gain that confidence was for me to coach them through their critical thinking on each coding decision. They'd be frustrated at first, but ultimately they would value their independence, and so would I.

So I started answering every question with a question:

"How were you thinking of coding that?"
"What keeps you from being confident that your instinct is correct?"
"What is it you are left wondering?"

I learned how people were thinking, where they were confident, where they weren't so confident. I never corrected people if they got on the wrong track—just asked more questions about risks they might not have anticipated. We talked through the risks of coding incorrectly and what might be done to mitigate them. By asking those types of questions, I was able to affirm their thinking and problem-solving capabilities. They got more confident, then more competent, and before long, they didn't need to ask me coding questions anymore. I had time to do the more important parts of my job—the parts that only I was qualified to do, like coaching and developing the managers under my supervision.

Principle 4: Forget Logistics and Focus Instead on Hearts and Minds

When you transition from managing to leading, the learning curve can be steep. When you're faced with new challenges, and it all feels like too much, you will be tempted to retreat to the realm of logistics and details—that place where you felt so comfortable as a manager. It's such a common reaction when the going gets tough for leaders. You are a great doer, but it's time to let others take care of logistics while you focus instead on presenting a compelling vision, thinking strategically about the future, and getting everyone in your organization to move forward in the same direction.

This tendency to demote oneself really comes from fear and lack of trust. We get into fight-or-flight mode and the stress hormone cortisol starts to call the shots. Then our inner control freak comes out, and we start telling everyone else how to do their jobs. When this happens, take a deep breath and know that your people are smart enough to manage the details for themselves. Remind yourself that engagement and happiness are correlated to personal responsibility, and that your people can't develop if you micromanage them.

If you tell yourself that no one else cares as much as you do, if you think that no one else can do the job quite the way you can, you are telling yourself a story. If you believe that story for long enough, and act as if others are incompetent, you will co-create that reality in your organization.

Principle 5: Allow People to Move Fully into Their Roles

If you are stalled in making the transition from manager to leader, it's probably because you have not allowed people to take full possession of their job titles and responsibilities. You are still holding onto the reins a little too tightly.

When we are promoted, sometimes it's tempting to hold onto some of our former duties—especially ones we like, in which we take particular pride. If you do this, you deprive someone else of the chance to prove himself. By the same token, when we promote people from within, we may tend to hold onto some ideas about them that are no longer true. For example, if an assistant in your organization moves up to the management level, colleagues may act bemused when he begins to assert his new authority. This is a natural reaction, but it isn't a generous or fair one. It undermines his confidence, telegraphing to him that you and his coworkers don't believe in his abilities.

If you have promoted someone and trained him in his new duties, make sure that he has a mentor to go to with any questions or problems, but don't rush in to correct or critique him every time he takes action—especially not in front of colleagues. Instead, encourage him by taking him seriously and letting him do his job. If there's a problem, take him aside or discuss it with his mentor. Work on building his confidence, and others will take your lead. His competence will grow. Your organization and the people within it must be flexible enough for job descriptions to change without undue editorializing. If it isn't, consider your role in creating and perpetuating that reality, and how you can encourage flexibility, without which it is impossible for people and company alike to grow.

Principle 6: Disregard Any and All Attempts at Emotional Blackmail

What do I mean by emotional blackmail? All the invalid conditions and objections people will bring up to play on your insecurities and manipulate you to argue or bargain with them. Here's what it sounds like:

> *"You haven't brought up this issue before."*
> *"This policy will probably change again tomorrow, so until it's definite . . ."*
> *"Well, you're the one who gets paid the big bucks."*
> *"I thought you of all people would know how to get us out of this mess. Guess I was wrong."*
> *"This is not the way things used to be."*

Statements like these have been remarkably effective at preventing leaders from insisting on a high standard of performance, continuous improvement, adaptability, and excellence. They also hook the ego, and that's dangerous territory. Often our first impulse on hearing statements like these is to argue or to start bargaining. Reality-Based Leaders simply refuse to do either—just as they refuse to argue with reality.

Arguing and bargaining are not good uses of your resources. They foster resistance and resentment. Besides, a leader does not need to justify or lower high expectations. If someone comes to you spoiling for a fight, don't let her engage you. Surrender—agree with what she is saying and act quickly to redirect her energy and focus to a more productive line of thinking.

Meet attempts at emotional blackmail with simple statements such as:

"Yes, you could be right."
"While that has been the standard in the past, here is how I would like you to do things now."
"That is true, and while we could focus on that, I would prefer that we focus on what will bring us the best results, and that is . . ."

Reality-Based Leaders turn the spotlight back by asking questions:

"What is your goal?"
"What are you doing to achieve it?"
"How's that working for you?"

If you feel pressured, surprised, emotional, or uncertain how to respond to someone, use what I call "the words of loving detachment":

"Wow."
"I see."
"Good to know."
"I'm learning a lot about you."
"You've given me a lot to think about."

These are my favorite management words, because they give you time to think, control your reactions, put your ego on ice, and avoid mirroring the emotions of others. Sometimes, your cool-headed response will be enough to reduce the temperature in the room. You acknowledge what people have said and redirect their energy in a more productive direction.

63

These practices have proven invaluable to me and to the executives I coach. Personal accountability, motivation, and happiness will increase as you adopt them in your office, and you will no longer have to wonder whether people see you as a manager or a leader.

CY'S BOTTOM LINE

If you feel you have to over-manage or micromanage, it is because you are under-leading.

Empowerment Without Accountability Is Chaos

By now, it should be obvious that a Reality-Based Leader cares about employees' opinions in direct proportion to what they contribute to the organization. So what do we do about the traditional employee satisfaction survey? It's almost blasphemy to suggest that these are useless documents. They started for a good reason: to find out how to better engage employees and empower them to do their best work. The problem with surveys, as they are used in most workplaces today, is that they don't measure accountability. Empowerment without accountability is chaos.

Traditional surveys are invitations for people to critique their reality, and, as such, they don't yield much useful intelligence. You usually get a lot more comments about the contents of your vending machines and your parking policy than you find useful. Without a foundation of personal accountability, all you end up with is a great list of what would need to change in order for your staff to grace you with their performance. In fact, many times you are simply surveying the victims. You tally the comments and make action plans that usually result in more work for managers and leaders: taskforces to spearhead, and things of that nature.

What are the odds of you creating, in today's world, the perfect environment in which your employees could work? Let's call them zero, just by general agreement. By setting up that expectation, you only set yourself up to fail. You can't create your employees' perfect environment, which gives them more gas for their BMWs—the bitching, moaning, and whining wagons—and ultimately leads to them quitting mentally.

The system is broken. The flawed assumption at the heart of the traditional employee survey is that all of the ideas and opinions you glean from these surveys are of equal value. The problem is that a certain percentage of your workers are low on personal accountability, and you only perpetuate their victim mindset by asking them to enumerate their complaints on a survey.

A Radical Approach: Survey for Accountability

If you simply must spend your time and resources on employee surveys, adopt a radical approach: survey not only for satisfaction, but for accountability—and weight the responses accordingly. This will enable you to give more credence to requests and critiques from your top performers and less to those from people in a mindset of resistance or learned helplessness.

If you are a leader who wants to dispense with time-consuming satisfaction surveys and implement this concept tomorrow, simply ask for each employee's response to two questions: "What is the one thing you need to be more productive in your work?" and then, "What are three things you are willing to do to get that which you have requested?"

For example, if an employee answers that he would need access to information and better communication from the leaders, he then has to identify three things that he will do to get it, such as ask for updates on a regular basis; when in doubt, make a phone call; and document what he does know in a knowledge management system and share with his coworkers. How's that for simple?

Eliminating the Victim Factor from Your Employee Survey

If you want your survey to be anonymous, or to look more traditional, here's a way to adapt one you are currently using. It's easiest to use the same format as the Alignment Survey in Appendix 1—the Likert scale of 1–5, in which 1 corresponds to "almost never," 3 corresponds to "sometimes," and 5 corresponds to "almost always." Take the questions you currently ask on your satisfaction survey, and add in some statements that measure accountability, such as:

1. I have participated in a development experience that was not funded or arranged by my organization in the past year.
2. Most employees have more influence on their supervisors than they think they do.
3. I am active in social networking and have more than 150 contacts.
4. For the issues that have come up in the past three months, I can identify at least three things I could have done differently to change the outcome.
5. Decision makers should take my opinion into account when making their decisions.
6. Employees need to be given time to adjust to changes in the organization.
7. The main difference between people who make a lot of money and people who make a little money is luck.

On the first four statements, you're looking for a high score—4s and 5s, ideally—to identify surveys from employees who are highly accountable. For questions 5–7, the opposite is true. A low score—1 or 2—on these questions indicates high accountability. Before you bother looking at the answers to any of your other survey questions, place the surveys in two categories: high and low accountability. Give more of your attention to those surveys that land in the first category. Read the others if you must, but you might as well file them in the circular file, for all the good they'll do your business.

If you have been trained in the traditional management value that it's not fair to play favorites, the idea of following this new model for surveys might make you uneasy—but it shouldn't. In Chapter Five, I explain why this is just another piece of insanity that holds your business back, and why playing favorites is a key strategy for Reality-Based Leaders.

ADDITIONAL RESOURCES: SELF-TEST

Turn to Appendix 2 for a test that will show you whether you have the right balance between managing and leading, and what specific aspects of leadership you most need to work on.

Play Favorites
Work with the Willing!

On any given day, if you get to the office with confidence, ready to engage fully with reality, you've won half the battle—but as a leader, you know that's the easy half. Enlisting other people is tougher than getting right in your own mind, and I'm willing to bet it's a challenge you meet on a daily basis. There are a lot of books out there on how to motivate people, but if you've ever tried to apply their advice, you know that the kind of person who responds best is usually the kind who was somewhat motivated already. There are always some people who won't sign up no matter how hard you try. They are the ones who can push you to the limits of your patience and resources.

Years ago, when I was struggling to win over some folks like that, my mentor asked me, "Cy, how many people do you have on your team?" I told her I had forty-one. She asked how many of them would go to battle for me, how many wanted success as much as I did. My answer? Three. She said, "I have an idea: start with them."

Work with the willing. It's the best advice I ever got, and in this chapter I break it down for you—showing you exactly why you should do it and how you can, starting today. "Working with the willing" doesn't mean ignoring everyone else. If I had tried to get my job done with just those three willing people while the other thirty-eight made chains out of paperclips, photocopied their body parts, and took three-martini lunch breaks, it would not have worked and I'd probably have been fired. So in this chapter, I also show you how to deal with everyone else. You won't be able to motivate them—we can't control other people that way—but you will be able to influence your office culture by focusing your attention on the people you want to reward. It all starts with a concept you probably haven't thought about since childhood: playing favorites.

Playing Favorites Is Fair Game

We have been conditioned since our nursery school days to think that playing favorites is unfair. Actually, if one of my young sons had a teacher who played favorites, I would not be thrilled. When we are small children, people in authority have a huge amount of influence over who we become, whether they fully accept that responsibility or not. Early in life, it's important that everyone be treated the same. But part of growing up is realizing that the world outside the nursery doesn't work that way; we *will* be treated differently based on our abilities, our aptitudes, and our attitudes. Will you ever forget the first time you tried out for something—a sports team, a youth orchestra, or the lead role in the school play—and didn't get chosen? Understanding why, and that it's less about fairness and more about effort and talent, is a big part of becoming an adult. By the time we get to the workplace, it is a lesson everyone should have absorbed. But in too many companies, it seems that the nursery rules have reasserted themselves.

Too many of the leaders I work with have surrendered to the idea of mediocrity in order to never, ever offend anyone. Some leaders are so concerned with treating everyone the same that they are hesitant to give honest feedback. Instead, they act as if all employees deliver equal results and value to their organizations, when the reality is quite different. They fear confronting underperformers, so they depend solely on a few great employees whom they don't reward, lest the others accuse them of unfairness or discrimination.

Reality-Based Leaders know that playing favorites is not only okay, it's great for the workplace. Protecting other adults from the results of their lackluster performance and unproductive mindsets is patronizing. You owe it to your colleagues to hold everyone to the same standards, to keep those standards high, and to reiterate them relentlessly. While it's never wise to favor an employee based on your own vanity (because you desire a "mini-me" for a protégé), and it's *never* okay—or legal—to discriminate based on race, physical abilities, sexual orientation, or religious affiliation, it *is* more than appropriate (and completely legal) to reward those who contribute the most to the success of your organization. Your best performers deserve a disproportionate share of your time and attention, so put aside any anxiety you might have over playing favorites in the office.

Identify the Visionaries

The first step to working with the willing is to identify the willing—which shouldn't be difficult. Luckily, around 20 percent of the workers in any given office are engaged, creative, and present. I call them the visionaries. They are personally accountable; they look for opportunities everywhere; they are resourceful and connected and optimistic. They look forward to coming to work, and they are your best people. But before you congratulate yourself, know that this has little to do with you. Visionaries, in most cases, come to you motivated and will stay that way unless you do something to demotivate them. Your big challenge with them is always retention. And that's where the other 80 percent of the people can really get in the way.

71

Unfortunately, in any given office, 20 percent of workers live in a permanent state of resistance. Everyone knows who they are. They walk around looking pained and miserable because their worldview is that the universe is unsafe and that everyone is out to get them. They bring their poor or ambivalent attitudes to every task. They get upset if you ask them to move their desks; they get upset if you change their job descriptions; offer them chocolate ice cream and you can bet they would have preferred vanilla. They're your toughest cases. At their worst, they can be bullies. (Is there someone who works under you that you are a little afraid of? Someone you spend a lot of time trying to avoid, or whose name comes up at your dinner table more often than you would like? That's who I mean.) At best, they're inaccessible to you: impervious to criticism and encouragement alike, and too complacent to find another job, they present a real leadership challenge.

The other 60 percent of workers in any given office are in survival mode—I call it maintenance, because they're not being proactive or making continual improvements. Instead, they're playing it safe. They get their work done, but they're always counting down the days to the weekend. Your people in maintenance are not working against you—but they won't show much enthusiasm and their effort is minimal and paycheck motivated. Many of them are the people in the Gallup poll I quoted in the Introduction, who consider quitting at least once a day. (But before you judge the people in maintenance who have quit in their minds but still come to work, think for a moment of the people you have fired in your mind but never told. They, too, keep coming to work and collecting a paycheck, much to the dismay of your top performers.)

Redirect Your Focus

Who Moved My Cheese? one of many famous books on getting people to adapt to change, focuses on survival—how to get past change and not complain about it when it inevitably happens. That's all well and good, but it's not exactly a place of greatness. But you're lucky to have those in maintenance, because they're the ones who maintain the status quo in your office by doing all the work you have to take away from the people in resistance. You reward their hard work with more work, but the problem is you didn't fire the people you took the work from. Having one foot out the door may not be ideal, but don't ever take your maintenance people for granted; they have the potential to change, and they can go either way—down to resistance with the bottom 20 percent, or up to vision with the top 20 percent.

Now, of the people in your office, who takes up most of your mental real estate? Would you be surprised to know that, on average, a leader will spend 80 extra hours each year thinking about and working with a single person who's in a chronic state of resistance?[1] The average return on this hefty investment is, at the most, 3 percent. I'm sorry to say that 3 percent doesn't account for other events with the power to transform people, like spiritual awakenings and near-death experiences.[2] If you factor those in, your odds of changing someone in resistance are close to zero. Why would we overestimate our ability to motivate people in resistance? It's that pesky ego again. We tend to ignore the people who are with us. We take them for granted. The ego is not as impressed with the people who validate us. On the other hand, the ego can't stand it when people are against us. So we direct our energy toward those resistant people, trying to get their help and approval. This is a waste of time.

If you focus your energy and attention on those in resistance, you are paying them to bully you, to critique and sabotage your plans—but that's not the bitterest fruit you will harvest when you plant this seed. The other people you lead will notice. They want attention, too, and you'll have shown them exactly how to get it. Before long, some of the 60 percent of your people who are in maintenance will be slouching low in their chairs, joining the resistant. Can you blame them?

But the worst is yet to come: after a while, your visionary 20 percent will be dying on the vine. They will get so frustrated with your office

73

culture that they will look for work elsewhere. It'll be easy for them to leave you, because they are friends with all the other visionary people in your industry. They're all down at the local climbing gym on the weekends, talking about where is a good place to work and where isn't. If you want them to stay and recruit their friends, play favorites—favor those who use their talents to work with, not against, your organization. Put your time and energy into training and developing your best people.

Compensate Value, Not Effort

One way to do this is to study both the research and current literature on success in business, along with the best employees in your organization, and notice the commonalities in mindsets and actions. Help your employees to develop similar competencies, and congratulate them when they do. Then, if it's up to you, take the next courageous step: compensate your best people in direct proportion to the value they deliver—not their effort, hours clocked, or daily tasks accomplished.

People will notice where your attention goes, and that's what you want to happen. In my work as a leader, I have often had employees say to me, "You play favorites!" To which I have always replied, "Why, yes I do. Would you like to be one of them?" I then follow up with a list of all of the competencies and behaviors that make some of my team members more beloved than others and the recipients of greater rewards than others. Some of those competencies and behaviors are being personally accountable, results driven, flexible, low drama, emotionally inexpensive, great with change, and supportive of the direction of the organization.

Make it absolutely clear what gets attention from you, and your impressionable people in maintenance will start to go where the love is. When you work with a group of willing people—no matter how small—you will start to get results that make believers of others.

You can even try some social engineering. Why not invite promising employees to join a book group in which you read and discuss books about how to be even more successful? Keep expanding the circle. Your visionaries will prove valuable in your quest to recruit others. If a colleague in vision approaches someone in maintenance and asks her to attend a special meeting or join an in-office book group, she will sign up very quickly. Attention from one of your office's star performers will outweigh any compliment you could pay her. Given the chance to join the ranks of the willing, people will either join joyfully or not, and both decisions should be fine with you. If you can get just 26 percent of your maintenance people into vision, you will tip the whole culture in favor of willingness. Then, those in resistance will opt out, either by choice or by behavior, and when 20 percent of your people quit, it will be the right 20 percent. But it won't happen immediately. In the meantime, there is a lot you can do to deal with people in resistance and avoid breeding more of them. Let's start with the latter.

Reality-Based Leadership, as a philosophy, has everything to do with recognizing and dropping limiting belief systems. When I go into a business as a consultant, I help the leaders to identify and understand what belief systems they are operating under that are holding them back and causing stress. A lot of times, those have to do with their talent decisions. I encounter many leaders who don't realize they are creating their own monsters.

If you have ever felt you were the victim of a past manager who handed down a group of problem employees; if you believe that giving feedback is not part of your job description; if you tend to shy away from the tough conversations that real leaders must have; read carefully: The reality is that you are creating the next generation of irrelevant, resistant employees with those beliefs. If you take the easy, cowardly way out, everyone suffers—but you suffer most of all. Your job is to make sure people sign up, or sign out.

CY'S BOTTOM
LINE
You will have problem employees for as long as you continue to hire them and put up with them.

Lack of Feedback Is the Root Cause of All Employee Issues

Employees who have bad attitudes or whose skills and abilities are irrelevant to your organization today were likely valuable employees once. Their irrelevance and resistance were, in part, created by leaders who were not relentless and consistent in giving feedback. To be clear: Lack of feedback is the root cause of all employee issues. Leaders who get lazy about giving development and performance feedback create resistant employees of many stripes. The three most common types:

1. *Tenured employees whose skills are not current.* This problem is created by leaders who do not challenge their employees to grow and develop by raising the bar for performance each year and offering new assignments. When job descriptions and responsibilities do not evolve over time, people stagnate and become bitter and unproductive.

The top 20 percent of employees will seek out such opportunities and hold themselves to a high standard of performance, but you can't rely on the other 80 percent to do that. If you do not consider mentoring and coaching part of your job description, you may end up with an office full of mediocre people who are no longer fully qualified to do their jobs but are too senior and/or too well behaved to fire.

2. *Employees at the top of their pay scale who no longer deliver top value.* This happens when leaders over-reward and under-coach employees over the course of their careers. Rewards start to seem like entitlements, and employees become convinced that they are far more valuable to your

organization than they are. They respond to coaching and criticism with resentment.

Every time you see someone underperforming and you ignore it, you set a new standard. If you are someone's manager, the first time the person underperforms, it is her performance issue, but if you fail to confront it, and it's still a problem months or years later, it has become your performance issue. If you are the sort of leader who loves to give feedback in the form of encouragement and rewards but hates to coach or criticize, beware of the long-term consequences: an office that runs on pure ego, full of people who can't imagine what you would do without them.

3. *Righteous top performers.* These are otherwise great employees whose contribution is compromised by their righteousness and judgment of others. Too many leaders allow—even encourage—their top performers to criticize other team members. They collude with these employees, granting them an inappropriate view into others' performance and their leadership decisions.

You are at particular risk of nurturing this brand of resistance if you have been promoted to a leadership position over your peers at work. Perhaps you feel a bit guilty—and they feel a bit jealous—about your new role. It will be tempting to show that you are still one of the gang by being indiscreet with them—resist! Working with the willing is not about forming a clique with your favorites and excluding others from the in-crowd.

The only way to avoid perpetuating these poisonous dynamics is to give frequent, honest performance and development feedback. Be consistent, be kind, and get it done. Don't wait for the yearly review; meet with your people one-on-one on a regular basis and keep detailed notes about their progress. It is vital that you get very clear about the mindsets and actions that will generate results for your organization. You will be contributing to a legacy of relevant, ready, and willing employees.

ADDITIONAL RESOURCES: FEEDBACK FRAME

In Appendix 3, you'll find a comprehensive feedback frame that you can use any time with your direct reports.

One-on-One Meeting Agenda

If you have a small team, it is ideal to plan a quick one-on-one with each of your people once a week. The benefit of this is that you keep abreast of any issues as they arise, so they don't metastasize, and your people always know when their next scheduled one-on-one is, so they can save up any noncritical questions for the meeting. Here's an example of what an agenda for such a meeting might look like:

Name:

Week ending:

What has been the most challenging part of your week?

What has been the most rewarding part of your week?

Goals or planned actions for the week:
1.
2.
3.

Progress on the goals or planned actions:
1.
2.
3.

Issues to review:

Resources needed:

Questions:

Next week's goals or planned actions:
1.

2.

3.

Additional discussion points:

The way to inspire loyalty is by being loyal yourself. Inspire optimism about the future by being optimistic yourself. Get respect by being respectful yourself. Embody the qualities you want to see in others. That is not simple advice, and I can't promise that it will always work. But I can tell you that if you are not loyal, optimistic, and respectful, you will never find those qualities in the people you lead. Living and working with integrity, in alignment with your own best values, is always worth the effort, whether or not others match it. More often than not, they will, because others' behavior toward us tends to work like a mirror.

Dealing with Resistance

In tough times and down markets, Reality-Based Leaders make it clear that buy-in is not optional—it's mandatory. The number one question I hear from my clients is, "How do I deal with resistant employees?" The answer is actually contained in the question: you *deal* with them, acknowledging their resistance and its costs to your organization. You don't ignore or avoid them and hope they will quit.

If you think you will always have issues with employees, you're co-creating that. If you see someone as a horrible employee, avoid him, and deprive him of straight feedback, what you get in return is a horrible employee who's still on your payroll. If you have employee problems, know that it's because you hired them or you continue to put up with them.

Resistant employees don't have to take up a lot of your time; however, they do take a great deal of managerial courage. When you lack the courage to address them rationally, clearly, and honestly, you will pay for it with a greater investment of time—and that becomes *your* choice and your problem, not theirs.

The best way to deal with a resistant person is to meet with him one on one and lay out your expectations and his options in a highly structured format. The reason I advocate structured meetings is that it will allow you to control your time investment in the resistant employee, avoiding rambling conversations and meetings in which nothing is accomplished. It will also leave you with a record of your coaching and the employee's response to it. These meetings are meant to be brisk and efficient, replacing the eighty hours you might have spent if you didn't use this coaching method.

In your first, very brief meeting, explain where the organization is going and what you are trying to accomplish. Invite the employee to take part. Tell him that you would love to have him on your team—but right now it feels like he is not signing up. Give one or two specific examples of how he has demonstrated his lack of commitment to the organization. Most employees, at this stage, will instinctively become defensive and begin to list excuses. You want to preempt that by asking questions that elicit accountability and invite constructive responses. Here is a constructive series of questions to ask a troubled employee:

- What is your goal at work?
- What has your approach been?

- How is that working for you?
- My observations of your approach have been . . . How far off am I?
- What would you like to change in your approach?
- What can you commit to today?

At the end of the first meeting, ask the employee to write a plan for how he can contribute more to the organization at less emotional expense. Set a deadline for him to turn it in to you and a date for a follow-up meeting. It is very important that the employee be the author of his plan. Resist the urge to spend a lot of your time doing it with or for him.

At your follow-up meeting, review his plan and make a decision. A plan that reflects willingness to accept personal accountability may be worthy of your investment of time and resources because it offers you the possibility of great returns. Continue to meet with the employee regularly while he is implementing the plan, to make sure he is on track. At these meetings, try these follow-up questions, depending on the progress you observe:

- What has led to your success in keeping your commitment?
- What plans are you making to ensure your success can be duplicated?
- What has kept you from fulfilling your commitment?
- What changes would you like to make in your approach?

If the plan does not have merit, or the employee has no plan, then it's time to begin planning his transition outside of your organization. You simply cannot afford a terminally resistant employee draining team and management resources, given the long odds that he will change. One very straightforward way to explain this to the employee is, "Your choices indicate whether or not you are choosing your way into our organization or out of our organization. I am simply observing your choices as they are made visible through your behavior." You will know you are in the danger zone if you are working harder at an employee's success than he is. These meetings should never be about what you can do for him but what he can do for himself.

You can't change a person. You can only invite someone to change. If you don't want someone on your team, or if you have made a hiring mistake, don't keep the person and torture him. Admit it—and pay severance. You'll both be better off if you are honest and you let him move on. Turnover is not necessarily a bad thing if you are losing the right people.

If you do have to let someone go, the upside is that you will have plenty of documentation and the decision won't come as a shock to the employee. People usually don't sue you for firing them; they sue you for how you made them feel. They sue you because you haven't offered them any feedback for a year and all of a sudden they're called into a conference room and given a cardboard box to pack their desks. This is just one more good reason to be consistent in giving feedback and to show compassion and respect at all times. If you treat everyone with compassion—especially the people you have to transition out of your organization—that little bit of kindness and effort goes a long way to mitigate anger and hurt feelings. It makes even the hardest conversations easier to bear.

Reality-Based Leaders devote their precious time and energy to teaching their employees how to succeed in spite of their circumstances. They work to "bullet-proof" people instead of attempting to make their world a safer place. Developing their resilience, agility, and personal accountability will increase their level of engagement, confidence, and satisfaction, especially in hard times.

Today's business environment can pose a challenge, even to the most habitually upbeat among us. In Chapter Six, I show you how Reality-Based Leaders bullet-proof their people to cope in times of change, whether they are changes within your organization, changes in the economy, or sudden crises no one can predict, like terrorism, a pandemic, or a natural disaster. Companies and individuals who see change as a source of opportunity are the ones who will not only remain resilient but will be genuinely visionary and thrive in challenging times.

6

Change Is a Fact of Life — Get Over It!
How to Bullet-Proof Your Employees

The ability to handle change is the best insurance policy money can't buy. It insulates us in hard times and enhances our performance in good times. If you prize flexibility—and everyone should—you will look at change as an opportunity or a practice to cultivate. Change is inevitable and impersonal, like the weather. It's an opportunity on which to capitalize; a whetstone to make us sharper. Yet our initial response to change is rarely constructive.

In a word, we tend to resist. Even changes we have anticipated, we greet with surprise. When change comes, we immediately feel threatened. We start to react, mentally, with stressful stories that we can't know to be true; and physically, with heightened blood pressure and adrenaline. We go through some predictable stages, all of which I'm sure you'll recognize:

Stage 1: Surprise

"You have got to be kidding me."

"This is unbelievable."

"Why me?"

Stage 2: Panic

"How does this affect me?"

"How will this look to our competitors and clients?"

"Can I do this? Am I competent?"

Stage 3: Blame

"It's all the [fill in the blank: boss's; media's; government's] fault."

"It's the economy, stupid."

"Our customers are just too demanding."

With ideas like these percolating in their minds, people naturally begin to fantasize about quitting their jobs. ("I don't have to put up with this.") I mean, what could be more natural? When faced with a situation that could be our greatest teacher, our first impulse is always to run. When we realize that quitting is unrealistic or impossible, we start daydreaming about a change of circumstances: everything everyone else should do to make our jobs easier. (That is when people start making those wish lists of extra resources I warned you about in Chapter Four: the ones only managers—not leaders—respond to.)

When people feel threatened, they retreat to the safest belief system they can find. "This stinks" is a nice one we can all dust off and repurpose from the last time we used it, circa third grade. "This won't work" is pretty useful, too, because it means we don't have to step up, make an effort, or be accountable for our results. Whatever the thought, in effect it takes them straight to resistance, where they congregate, loitering and complaining, drinking your free coffee, and gathering fuel from other people's stories and gossip. This is the default setting on dealing with change in most organizations, and it is the worst-case scenario. When people waste their energy on surprise, panic, blame, fantasy, and complaints, they are not giving their talent, and they are not innovating. You might as well send them home, because they are a drain, costing more than they contribute.

84

I can promise you one thing: change isn't going anywhere, but your job just might if you don't learn to handle change constructively. Organizations that survive and thrive during times of change have leaders and employees with three things in common. In this chapter, I give you examples of each of these core competencies and methods for cultivating them in yourself and those you lead. I signpost three common mistakes to avoid. Last, I share my best practices for leading people through a crisis. Acts of God, headcount reductions, epidemics, and strikes can happen at any time, so it pays to be prepared.

Three Core Competencies That Make People Bullet-Proof

If you want to protect your organization from learned helplessness and set it up for success, regardless of changing circumstances, there are three competencies you must work on.

Competency 1: The Ability to Respond to Adversity

The ability to respond to adversity is all about greeting change with courage, skipping the surprise, panic, blame, and complaints. Reality-Based Leaders always greet change with a simple phrase: "Good to know." Then they move on right away to understand their new reality and search for ways to deliver results. Any other response constitutes an argument with reality and invites others to waste their time and creative energy doing the same. "Good to know" is similar to the words of loving detachment you learned in Chapter Four, in that it allows you to ignore the first few (usually unconstructive) thoughts that enter your mind and gives you a neutral place from which to plot your next move.

Many organizations miss the opportunity to capitalize on a changing world and instead curse the change forever—which is like cursing the wind for blowing from a different direction instead of working to quickly

85

readjust the sails. Capitalizing on change requires a leader with an open mind, one who isn't mired in a mindset of "I know what is right."

The administrative team in a regional hospital began to notice that physicians were being faced with some tough circumstances:

Declining reimbursement levels from payers
Less control over their own income levels
Increased reliance on complex hospital systems with decreased ability to influence regionally
Inability of hospitals to provide the necessary capital for newer surgical suites
Higher expectations from patients for convenience, additional amenities, and less complicated admission procedures

The physicians began to openly discuss their vision for a new model of care—a surgery center built across a state border (advantage: no state income tax) in a new, quickly developing high-end area. At the new center, they could separate out the complex surgeries from more routine procedures, giving patients a quicker, more convenient option for same-day surgery in a facility that felt more like a hotel than a hospital.

The center would eventually become a mini-hospital in which the physicians would be investors and secure their own incomes by diversifying their income streams. As owners, they would have a say in all the crucial decisions that affected their working lives.

Two major health centers, already well established in the area, were threatened by the new model, even if it was essentially just a same-day surgery center. They feared that the new center would cherry-pick the best cases—patients needing the least complex, most insured surgeries with the highest likelihood of good outcomes. This would leave the two established hospitals with the most complex cases, adversely affecting their outcome statistics and sticking them with the costs of treating the uninsured and underinsured.

One hospital vowed to fight, refusing to support the physicians and even building its own surgery center at a cost of millions of dollars. This center was undersubscribed, duplicated services, and wasted community resources.

The other hospital moved quickly from resistance to working to understand the new model, doing its best to see the situation from the physicians' perspective. The physicians would be meeting a legitimate need in the community—one welcomed by patients. They would be improving their own situation as well. The one element the new model was missing was care for more complex cases and vital emergency room support for the safety of their day-surgery patients, should a procedure go awry. The hospital found some common ground with the physicians, who understood that they had a vested interest in keeping the hospital healthy if their model was to succeed long term.

While the first hospital chose to fight for the status quo and protect itself from the "threat" of the new center, ultimately losing both money and goodwill among the physicians and within its community, the second hospital looked for opportunity and was able to exploit it to a competitive advantage. Hospital staff met with the physicians and validated, rather than criticized, the physicians' goals as natural, their motives as benevolent. They proposed a joint venture in which the hospital could provide capital to the new center and enter into a joint planning process, so that it could best equip the old main campus surgery suites with nonduplicative but necessary new robotic equipment.

The two entities even agreed on how to choose patients and where patients could receive services. Ultimately, the more flexible hospital made money from surgeries done off its campus—a great return on their investment. The hospital was more financially diversified, had a great understanding of its competition, and was seen as progressive and friendly to physicians. In addition, the hospital mitigated the risk of losing services in the community while wisely choosing not to duplicate services. This was one of the best examples I have seen of the competency of responding to and capitalizing on adversity.

Competency 2: A Profound Commitment to Succeed in Spite of the Facts

Once you have taken the measure of your new reality and accepted it with a simple "Good to know," your next commitment is to succeed in spite of the facts. No situation is ever perfect, but by choosing your reaction carefully you signal your intention to work with what you have.

The point of bullet-proofing is not simply to greet change without complaining. When someone is wearing a bulletproof vest, the impact of a bullet may not kill him, but it doesn't mean he won't feel some pain and surprise. A shot may knock him to the ground and take his breath away. But he can recover quickly, so he has the opportunity to do far more than merely survive.

If you can move quickly beyond that first all-too-human resistance to change, you can start discussing possibilities and opportunities to capitalize on the change while your competition is still stuck in the "Why me?" phase. The organization that sees change as an opportunity is the one whose talent is going to lead it well into the future.

Bulletproof employees use change to their advantage.

Negative Brainstorming

One of the most useful tools for transitioning a team from resistance toward succeeding in spite of their circumstances is called "negative brainstorming." You'll need a whiteboard or a big flipchart to get started. Here's how it works.

First, the rules: each individual can introduce his or her concerns, one at a time, in front of the group, while you write them down (leaving ample space in between for the next step in the exercise). The other members of the group must refrain from discussion, critique, or disagreement and wait their turns. Continue until the group has exhausted their list of concerns and all concerns are documented.

Title the list of concerns "Risks." Point out that all concerns are simply risks and the true power of the team lies in their ability to mitigate risks. This idea is at the heart of the exercise—and the reason it works.

Taking it risk by risk, ask the team to honestly evaluate the probability of each risk manifesting itself. Assign each a probability of High, Medium, or Low. Next, evaluate the potential impact of each risk and again label it High, Medium, or Low.

Now comes the negative brainstorming. Redirect all the energy that the team was putting into resistance or dissent and harness it to create strategies to mitigate each risk that is of Medium to High probability or impact.

Teams that can move from using their expertise to resist and editorialize and instead use those same talents and expertise to "make it work" are the teams that successfully position themselves as valuable assets and credible witnesses. That's why it can be positive to get negative with your team—but in the service of moving them forward, creating great results, and succeeding in spite of challenging circumstances.

When you trust people with this kind of exercise, it shows your faith not only in their talents but also in their good intentions. Negative brainstorming provides Reality-Based Leaders with a constructive way to get concerns out on the table and give dissent a place within a healthy team dynamic. It's an especially great tool to keep leading constructively even when your company has done something you, the leader, do not like. It's tempting to stop leading under those circumstances, but instead—once again—your responsibility is to redirect everyone's focus. (You go first!) In the end, it's all about the overarching vision of what you have joined together to create, because risks are here to stay. Your perspective is what matters.

> Two customer support centers were about to merge. One center would be closing and their work transitioning to another site. The workers in the defunct center would be responsible for training their replacements and would have the opportunity either to move across the country or to take on a role in collections, which many saw as a step down in the hierarchy.
>
> As you might imagine, they went through the typical reactions—surprise, panic, and blame. Their leader was honest with them, but he kept his focus solely on how they could succeed at what the company was asking of them in spite of their circumstances. The opportunity in front of them was to knock the socks off the company during the transition process. If they committed wholeheartedly to what they were being asked to accomplish, the powers that be would see how committed and professional the team was. Whether or not they chose to stick with the company post-transition, each team member would have an amazing story to tell at his or her next job interview. The leader won

them over to the idea, and whenever they would start to slip, he would remind them of their commitment to their own professionalism and to the company they worked for—even if only for a short time. The tool he used most often to redirect them from the negative to the positive, and to succeeding in spite of the facts, was negative brainstorming.

The risks they identified in their situation were these:

- Morale will stink.
- Too much time will be spent on complaining rather than helping.
- We could all end up without jobs.
- Many of us can't move because of family situations.
- Some employees may leave early and a few of us will be left in the lurch, responsible for the whole transition.

Then they identified ways in which they could mitigate those risks:

- They would call "huddle meetings" every two hours to keep people pumped up and the focus on success.
- They would highlight and reward the most positive individuals by starting a résumé for each employee on the shared drive. When someone did something showing a great competency, anyone (especially supervisors) could add the recognition directly to their résumé for future use.
- They put together retention bonuses for those who would stay.
- They enlisted a network of connections to meet, during business hours, with job seekers who needed to transition out of the company.

In the end, all who wanted to find jobs did, and a core group went on to form a specialist "transition" team for the company. Because of their amazing show of talent during that first tough transition, they thereafter got to be the team that implemented all the big, highly visible strategic projects for the company. This led to whole new careers for them—ones much more valuable and highly paid than their former positions in customer support.

Competency Comes After Confidence

In order to succeed in spite of your circumstances, you have to tap into belief. Whether you believe something is possible or impossible, you will be right. Competency comes after confidence, not before. Confidence is what Reality-Based Leaders build through changing mindsets and inquiring on untrue stories, as you learned to do in Chapters Four and Five. Competence comes only after people buy in emotionally, because the learning brain is subordinate to the emotional brain. If people are not engaged, they can't accomplish a thing. How they see their situation affects their actions, and by extension, their outcomes.

Here's a real-life example to illustrate the point. I took a project team and briefed them on their budgets, their deliverables, their time frames, and what I expected of them. Then I took each of them aside privately to ask if they thought it would be possible to meet those expectations in time and on budget. Some of them said "No" and some said "Yes." I divided the team into two groups, each with the same level of talent and proficiency, working on the same project under the same circumstances. The only difference was that Group A was comprised of all those people who said "Yes" and Group B of those who said "No." Group A, the group with the belief that it was possible, delivered what I requested on time, under budget. Group B has not delivered to this day. I have repeated this experiment over and over and over again, in different companies, to prove to leaders that great results are not about circumstances. In fact, whenever I get to choose my own project teams within a company, I use this technique to choose according to belief rather than technical skills. I refuse to end up with the super-smart technical geek who has no confidence the project can work. Technical skills are far less valuable to me than belief. All else being equal, the teams that pull off the greatest challenges are those who believe that they can.

If people are having trouble finding the opportunity in a challenge, start from the assumption that the universe is benevolent, and ask them to list at least three reasons that what is happening could be for the higher good. Focus on those ideas and invest energy and talent to make sure that they come to fruition. Use your warm, fuzzy skills to inspire cold, hard results.

Competency 3: The Will to Resolve and Move Through Conflict Very Quickly

Tapping into emotion is essential to belief, but I want to draw a distinction between constructive and destructive emotional responses. If you are a lover of drama, or you recognize this tendency in those you lead, put a lid on it. If you encourage people to look at their challenges from a melodramatic perspective ("It's us against the world!" "We'll show them!"), you encourage a victim mentality. Why? To see your department, your team, or your company as embattled requires an enemy or an aggressor. People can become addicted to the adrenaline rush of conflict, to the point that they need to feel beleaguered in order to perform. They're being reactive instead of proactive. Over time, that's destructive and leads to resentment and burnout.

Being a lover of resolution, on the other hand, leads to joy and engagement. When resolution is your ultimate goal, you move very quickly through conflict without getting mired in it. That's the third core competency you must cultivate in order to thrive in times of change. One of the coaching techniques I like to use for dispelling conflict is an exercise in compromise that takes its cue from a simple shift in vocabulary: from *or* to *and*. All-or-nothing thinking is a common source of conflict, and most of the time it is unnecessary, as you'll see in the following example.

I was called in to consult for a hospital administrator who was at her wit's end with a feud between her lab director and the referring physicians. The lab director was working toward the hospital's goal of cost cutting through increased efficiency, and her plan for meeting this goal was to run tests in bigger batches and eliminate the many "one-offs" that were run at the request of the physicians, wasting materials that couldn't be reused and utilizing staff time inefficiently. This change of the lab director's policy had led to slower turnaround times for lab results.

The physicians were furious. They wanted the convenience of quick lab results—both for their patients and themselves. The battle between the physicians and the lab director had come down to convenience *or* efficiency.

I first helped them identify their common goal, which was great patient care. I then identified the smaller goals of convenience and efficiency. By replacing *or* with *and*, the question changed. I asked them to identify ways in which they could enhance efficiency while maintaining convenience as needed. This small change of wording— *or* to *and*—opened up a whole new world of possibilities.

They decided each physician would be allotted "Monopoly money"—$10 per week that they could use, at their discretion, to quick-order tests, maintaining convenience (and their ability to make the final decision) in the most urgent situations. The lab knew the extent to which their plans would vary. With a guarantee of no more than ten one-offs per physician per week, they could better manage efficiency and expenses. In the end, both goals—efficiency and convenience—were served. The physicians ran far fewer one-off tests than they had imagined they would as they adjusted to the new system. This technique can also be applied on a larger scale to move people forward when problem solving.

Thinking Inside the Box

Most of the solutions we are called upon to provide on a daily basis involve finding a way forward given competing priorities or limited resources. After having been encouraged to "think outside the box" for many years, you may have come to overuse this competency or use it at inappropriate times. The time for thinking outside the box is during strategic planning efforts or business process reengineering efforts. Consistently ignoring your organization's constraints and providing "out of the box" thinking in problem-solving efforts is a big mistake. You will come to be seen as "pie in the sky" or out of touch with reality.

Instead of thinking about all the things that shouldn't be happening or thinking of the ideal situation *for you*, recognize and accept your company's goals and constraints (such as frozen headcount or limited funding) and *think inside that box*. The constraints are real—wishing them away won't help—but you can propose solutions that address them while also serving your goals. Again, think in terms of *and*, not *or*. By doing this you will be offering real solutions that respect the very real constraints you currently face.

Exercise

When you can see that employees are wishing away their current reality and need to be able to imagine ways they could achieve their goals given their constraints, try this step-by-step exercise with them, moving them from a sense of lack and impossibility to focusing on solutions.

1. Identify the goal or goals.
2. Identify the constraints or competing needs.
3. Box it out.
4. Replace *or* with *and*.
5. Problem-solve.

People with these three competencies—the ability to respond to adversity; a profound commitment to succeed in spite of the facts; and the will to resolve and move through conflict very quickly—are invaluable. These people are clear about their purpose, and they're able to align their efforts with your organization with very little hand-holding. These people are not just with you for a paycheck. These, again, are your visionaries, who can drive for results. If you look for employees who have these competencies, regardless of their functional expertise, you will benefit from their ability to turn their talent into productivity.

Three Common Mistakes to Avoid

I prefer to accentuate the positive, but experience has shown me that under changing circumstances, leaders tend to make certain tactical errors again and again. They're patterns that are hard to recognize when you're in them, but I hope that if I lay them out for you, you'll cultivate your awareness and be able to avoid them in the future.

Mistake 1: Lying

The first mistake that I see many people make when a change is being rolled out is lying to people. We don't think of it as lying, exactly, but that's what it is. We are concerned about people's reactions to the truth, and so we tend to leave things out or gloss the situation over. We say things like:

> "You are going to love this new system when you get the hang of it!"
> "This will be great for our customers."
> "It won't be long before everyone's up to speed and more efficient than ever before."

What we really need to do in the beginning is be honest with people. If you sense people are in denial, over-communicate. We should be saying things like:

> "For three to four months you're going to struggle, but things will get better."
> "This will require extra work from everyone, but here are some of the benefits that we are hoping will make it worth it . . . "
> "Although this situation is not ideal, I can't help but feel confident with such a competent group of people to implement the new system."

If you're honest about the difficulties ahead, highlight long-term benefits, and communicate your confidence that everyone is up to the challenge, you're telling people a very different story—one they can believe in.

Mistake 2: Trying to Reason with Anger

Sometimes, when people are blindsided by changing circumstances, they react with anger. It's a perfectly valid reaction, and the thing to

95

remember is that it's not personal and it's not forever. They will get over it.

When people get angry, do not indulge them. Instead of trying to talk them out of it, which is ego-driven and only fuels the fire, use scripted responses like "Oh" and "Wow" and "You've given me a lot to think about." Encourage them to come back and speak to you when they are calm. Let them know that, while it's okay to have anger, it's never okay to be unprofessional with anger. You may empathize, but there are limits to the behavior you will tolerate. They—not you—are in charge of managing their emotions.

Beyond that, you should not have to do or say anything more. When their fury burns itself out, people will most likely be mortified and eager to move on. If they don't move on, make your expectations clear one more time: they either catch up to their team's vision, or catch the bus.

Mistake 3: Dropping Support

The last mistake many leaders make is supporting their people during implementation of a change only to drop their support immediately after. So it doesn't stick. Usually, leaders are so exhausted from doing the change cycle wrong that they abandon their people just when they are most needed. You need to offer twice as much support post-implementation: pointing out key wins, thanking your top performers, and highlighting the efforts and the kinds of behavior you want to see in the future.

Best Practices in Times of Crisis

In our lifetimes—even within the past decade—we have witnessed economic downturns with mass layoffs, terrorist attacks, natural disasters, and the threat of pandemic flu. The world is a complicated place, and we have to accept that we have no control over it. In times of crisis, the best Reality-Based Leaders can do is be prepared. All of my earlier advice about bullet-proofing still applies, but when uncertainty reigns and people are panicking with some cause (for once), it takes a special kind of leadership to keep them on track.

Dealing with Impending Layoffs

I'll start with the most common crisis we face these days: impending layoffs. What do you do when you can't change a declining situation and people's jobs are threatened (possibly yours, too)?

The number one thing you can do is focus on others. Show you care about them. Be present and be trustworthy. Don't lie, justify, collude, or argue with people. Tell them everything you know and be honest about what you don't know. Strip what you share down to facts, leaving out rumors and gossip. It won't be news to them anyway, and you'll only contribute to a culture of fear about what may be happening. Listen to their fears and empathize, but then redirect them. Phrases like this might help:

"This seems to be the way of it."

"Yes, things are changing."

"You are right, that is different from what we heard yesterday."

"Yes, this does seem hard to trust."

"I hear you."

If you are not in the position of decision maker, offer expertise, not editorials.

Editorializing about decisions made by another level of the leadership team is a cardinal sin. There are no perfect decisions; all decisions have one or many downsides. The highest use of your talent and energy is to help identify any risk posed by a decision and rally your team around mitigating that risk.

When you redirect, help people get their focus out of the future—where all their most stressful stories live—and on the present, where they can have an impact and feel confident. Get their attention on what they know for sure today; what they need to do their jobs well today:

> "Today, we have jobs."
> "No, we don't know what we will hear tomorrow. But today, here is where I would like you to focus."
> "Today, we have customers, and we have a commitment to do a great job for them, so let's start there."
> "Today, let's work so we can be proud of what we accomplished."

Remind them that they are talented, smart, capable people and that you are confident that they can handle anything that comes their way. If you need to transition someone out of the company, treat him with respect, help him reframe and see his opportunity so that he can leave strong, ready for his next step. If he is angry, emotional, or resentful, you may have to absorb that, but remain empathic, respectful, and kind. If you do these things, you will be able to look back on a tough time and be proud of the way you led. If you, too, must move on, you'll be able to do so with a clear conscience, knowing you did your best. That's all anyone can ask of us.

If you are in a declining situation over which you have influence, you may be faced with the decision of who stays and who goes. There are no perfect decisions at a time like this, but my best advice is—if at all possible—to choose according to talent rather than title. It is shortsighted to make cuts solely based on positions that no longer serve the highest good for the organization. Instead, assess your talent and use headcount reductions as an opportunity to say good-bye to talent that is resistant or stagnant, and keep employees who are high performing, agile, and vision-ary because they will be willing and able to serve in a variety of capacities.

If you are in a position that truly merits a decrease in head count, cut a bit deeper than the budget calls for, so that you can recoup more resources to reward, recognize, and develop the top talent that you have chosen to keep. Such foresight will ensure that you are better able to retain and develop your best people while reducing their risk for burnout.

I always advise my clients, when considering headcount reductions, to think in terms of the income statement, not the balance sheet, because the income statement measures the true return on investment. All costs are not created equal in their potential to generate income. The same dollar cost can return significantly different levels of value, depending upon where in the organization it is invested. Simply balancing the books, matching cost against budget dollars available, doesn't take that into account. Instead, cut those expenses that are delivering the lowest return.

Conventional wisdom dictates that downsizing efforts focus on the non-revenue-generating portion of a business, leaving any commission-based sales force intact, since it would appear that there is little downside to having a large, underproducing sales force. Conventional wisdom is wrong in this case, as in so many others. Salespeople do carry a cost over and above their commissions—the cost of supporting and managing them. Depending upon their volume, your return on investment varies greatly. Also, keeping a huge sales force can lead to wasting syndrome, in which too many people are fighting for the same sales and all are starving. Your best people will quickly realize the lack of prospects and leave. Those less confident in their ability to produce anywhere else will stay, thus ensuring that you not only have a smaller sales force, but one made up of mediocre performers. You are better off cutting even commission-only sales people to concentrate on top performers, insisting that they reach higher goals and then compensating them accordingly.

Dealing with Emergencies and Disasters

We've discussed some of the worst moments that can happen inside your organization. Unfortunately, the world outside holds even scarier possibilities. Here is some guidance on leading during external crises, such as terrorist attacks, natural disasters, or pandemics. Whether or not the worst happens on your watch, preparing for every contingency means you will be golden when sudden, yet mundane, events (like transit strikes or snowstorms) threaten to interrupt productivity.

In a situation like this, gather the facts available, but avoid hiding out in your office, watching the news. You have a job to do, and that's to keep everyone calm and concentrate on what you can all know to be true. In the beginning, that may be very little. But the 24-hour news cycle breeds panic, Chicken Little–style overreactions, and speculation, not wise action. Wise action is what's needed, so get out of your office and go where people can see you and be influenced by your stability.

Your goal in any potential crisis is to mitigate the risks to employees while continuing to provide the best possible service to customers. Black-and-white, all-or-nothing thinking will not help you with this; complications are to be expected and taken in stride.

Begin by identifying critical functions of your business from the point of view of the customer (such as phone sales, order fulfillment, and product service). Identify the non-customer-facing support on which these functions depend (such as human resources, shipping and receiving, admin and tech support). Have each employee either write down or create a YouTube video of their critical functions, creating a low-budget training tool you can use, if needed, in their absence. This is excellent documentation to have in any case.

The lack of knowledge transfer is a great risk to every business, so use this as an opportunity to heighten the urgency of such behavior. If you want to take it even further, have each employee train another in their job in order to earn a bonus and certification. A simple reward system can buy a great deal of risk mitigation, which is extremely valuable to the business while motivating the employees to document their expertise.

In ordinary times, most companies are grouped by function, but that system leaves whole functions at risk. In an emergency, it is smarter to separate people into new teams that cover the entire customer experience and can be duplicated throughout the organization. That way, if an entire team falls ill, or a critical player in one area is unable to get to work, you still have multiple other complete teams to fall back on. Segregate your teams to different locations or different floors, make use of creative schedules, even segregate elevators if necessary in the case of contagious diseases like the flu. You can decide upon—and drill—these teams in advance if you like, much as you do your twice-yearly fire drill.

Keep the option of sending employees home as a last resort. To prepare for that contingency, implement technology that will allow people to fill customer needs virtually, if possible. If you must send people home, keep it simple. Ask every employee to create a plan for how they will work from home if necessary, and to create a phone chain, with one employee calling another down the list. Larger companies should set up an emergency number employees can call for recorded updates on whether the company is open or shut and what actions to take.

The truth is, leaders need to work to mitigate risk every single day, not just when disaster looms. When routine breaks down, poor leadership is quickly exposed. My advice for emergency preparedness differs only slightly from my general advice to Reality-Based Leaders. The key to success in a crisis is an attitude ingrained in organizations on a daily basis—not just a plan to apply at the last minute.

The advantages of planning for a crisis (even when there isn't one) are many. Employees will understand the way your organization fits together, learn job functions adjacent to their own, develop loyalty to peers who are affected by their decisions, and increase their appreciation for the overall customer experience. You'll have comprehensive job descriptions to help you train new people, and you'll begin to feel confident that if things fall apart, you'll all be in it together, supporting one another and doing your best to keep business moving forward in spite of your circumstances. You might not appreciate the results of your work in this area until a crisis shows you just how strong your people are.

Lead Your Team to Results

Up until now, I have offered you strategies for changing your own mindset and for coaching others, one on one, to do the same. In Part Three, you will learn how to apply Reality-Based Leadership concepts to working with teams: to implement plans with excellence, break through resistance and excuses, solve long-term problems, and make your office the kind of place where everyone—including you—wants to work.

I explain why much of what you may have learned in the past about leading teams no longer applies and may even be limiting your progress. I show you how to adopt strategies that do work and how to get your teams working efficiently as a single organism, toward results in which you can all take pride.

7

Opinions No Longer Count — Actions Do!

I hope that you now have a deeper understanding of how Reality-Based Leadership can contribute to your happiness, success, and influence and add to the tools you need to return peace and sanity to your workplace. Peace comes when you stop your argument with reality, and sanity comes when you help those around you do the same. Part Three is about using Reality-Based Leadership to drive results. Peace and sanity alone, while highly desirable, will not bring you results. If only it were that simple!

Limiting Beliefs That Hold You Back

You have probably observed that you don't necessarily need peace and sanity in order to get results. Most of the people I work with are very successful, but they have achieved their success with a high degree of self-inflicted stress, chaos, and insanity. I help them tap into their highest potential with the skills discussed in Parts One and Two. Once those skills are in place, we uncover people's limiting beliefs: the ideas they think they know for sure that are holding them back.

Chances are, there are many ideas you have internalized about leadership that are no longer relevant to the business climate in which you currently work. Everyone has some limiting beliefs, and when you identify and stop acting on yours, those you lead will respond with a higher level of engagement, ownership, and performance.

In this chapter, I identify seven of the most common limiting beliefs and talk you out of them, showing you how they all lead to one conclusion: action is what counts in getting results. When you lead a team with that in mind, you will realize that practically everything else amounts only to stress and noise. I start with the most basic.

Limiting Belief 1: Everyone's Opinion Counts

Human Resources gospel has always been to make employees feel as if their opinions counted. After all, this is America, and democracy is a good thing, right? Not always.

Your workplace is not a democracy. We know the value of democracy in a representative government, but what value does an opinion contribute to your organization? If you think you are having a heart attack, and you race to the emergency room, do you care what the receptionist thinks is wrong with you? Or do you wait for the cardiologist?

Ninety percent of people in any organization at any given time are not key decision makers. Their role is to implement decisions to the best of their ability, not to comment on them. If you subscribe to the idea that everyone's opinion has to count, in effect you are handing out veto power to the majority when only a minority has the power to say "Yes." This sets up a paradigm in which it's very difficult to take positive action. You create a situation in which people feel buy-in is optional. This leads to resistance that can stall or even sabotage your plans. Reality-Based Leaders are clear that the highest value the talent under their leadership can offer is to implement decisions with excellence. They value action over opinion.

If you are a decision maker faced with making plans that others will implement, you may wish to consult with people who have relevant expertise and experience. But avoid gathering opinions for the sake of inclusiveness. The opinions of people with no relevant expertise are of no value to you. They will be superfluous at best, counterproductive at worst. Does this mean that you don't care about these people as valuable members of the team? Absolutely not. And that's just one of several good reasons not to encourage them to editorialize about decisions and instead make it clear to them that their action—in executing the plan, mitigating its risks, and making it work for your customers—is far more valuable to the company.

Just because you are a leader in your organization doesn't mean you will always be in the position of decision maker. If you are ever uncertain whether you—or someone else—is truly the decision maker, the key question to ask yourself is, "Do I have the authority to say Yes as well as No?" Many people in an organization may claim veto power (after all, "No" is often a safer answer than "Yes"), but authority to say "Yes" is what truly marks a decision maker.

At times, you might be charged with implementing plans that you did not design—plans you might even dislike or view as flawed. It will be tempting in those situations to make a half-hearted effort instead of giving it your all, to tell yourself there is no way you can do what is being asked of you, that you wouldn't even know where to start. To deliver results time after time, leaders—just like those they lead—need to resist editorializing.

When a plan comes down from on high, most people's first impulse is to waste their time on drama—"Why wasn't I consulted?" But in today's climate of fast-paced change and intense competition, a team that can take that plan and direct their considerable energy and talent to making it work is the team delivering true value. What they will get in return, aside from respect and job security, is credibility. Offering your opinion of a plan before you have made it work is just useless editorializing. However, after you and your team have achieved the desired results, your opinion counts as feedback. You may be accustomed to think of feedback as primarily between boss and employee regarding performance. That is one useful type of feedback. But in this context, decision makers will be looking for other kinds of feedback—not only from outside the company (their customers and their market), but from those within the organization who are great implementers and can advise them on how to get the job done faster, better, or cheaper than before. Being consulted on decisions is an honor and a privilege you and your team must earn through your actions.

If you are asked for feedback about a plan, know that the decision maker is asking for your expertise—not editorials. Proactively offer up a variety of ideas. Outline the potential benefits of each course of action along with the corresponding risks, complete with your team's plan to mitigate the risks of any chosen option. Resist the urge to favor one option over another or to push your own agenda. Make it clear to the decision maker that you and your team are committed to deliver on any option chosen.

Criticizing any decision made by another level of your leadership team is a cardinal sin. If your team members can tell that you are not supportive of a decision even though you're heading the implementation plans, you have failed them in one of the worst possible ways. If you don't buy in and offer up your best effort, why should they? They will feel conflicted every day as they try to implement a plan that you have already told them (whether in so many words or not) isn't worth their effort. This leads us to a second common limiting belief.

Limiting Belief 2: Great Results Can Only Come from Perfect Plans

Whether a plan is your own or comes from another level of leadership, it will always entail a certain amount of risk. There are no perfect plans or decisions—all have one or many downsides. It is a poor use of your time to try to perfect a plan that can never be faultless. A better use of your team's talent and energy is to help anticipate any problems and rally around finding solutions before they manifest.

Having acknowledged the risks inherent to your plan, you must stay flexible and open to new information. Part of implementation with excellence is being willing and ready to adapt your course rapidly if outside intelligence offers you an opportunity to refine your strategy. Keeping consistently alert to new possibilities and realities is integral to Reality-Based Leadership. The best plans are flexible and adaptable—never perfect. The surest way to fail is to decide that you already know everything.

It seems like every time I read the news or watch the CNN crawl from an airport lounge, leaders are rehearsing their stories: reasons and excuses for why they aren't getting the results they desired or even the results they promised. They don't even have to be creative or dishonest in their attempts to justify their shortcomings. We all know their reasons: too few resources, talent shortages, increased regulation, declining margins, losses on investments, decreased consumer confidence and demand. But these reasons hold true for nearly every sector and situation. More often than not, none of these justifications is the real reason for their poor results. Poor results can nearly always be traced back to poor execution.

There are two distinct camps in the business world today: leaders whose teams have failed to measure up, who work diligently to deliver the "facts" in the form of reasons, stories, and excuses, and leaders whose teams have delivered results in spite of the same "facts." The difference between these two camps lies not in their circumstances but in the path that the leaders chose to take. Check out the Results Circle in Figure 7.1 for a graphic illustration of the consequences of each approach.

Each half of the circle represents a path a leader can choose. The upper left-hand side represents accountability; the upper right-hand side represents the blame and collusion that follow when you don't take

Figure 7.1 Results Circle

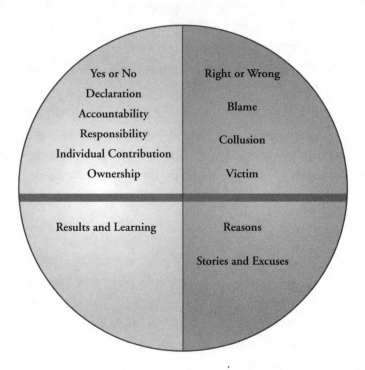

responsibility and instead choose to see yourself as a victim. The lower part of the circle shows the results of each approach: Results and Learning versus Reasons, Stories, and Excuses. Here's how it works.

The path leading to reasons, stories, and excuses begins when a leader decides that he is right, that his plan is perfect (or someone else's is flawed), and that he knows how things are or how they should be. Once he starts judging, in effect he stops leading and is no longer adding value. This hubris usually arises from past successes mistakenly attributed to his infallibility rather than to the execution and risk mitigation of his team (or sheer luck, always a possibility). The problem with this attitude is that nothing out in the world is static or even predictable. The minute you are convinced your way is fail-proof, you close your mind and become righteous. You are no longer open to new or contradictory information that could help you improve or correct your plan and execute it successfully.

When a leader is invested more in being right than in getting results, a great deal of his energy is diverted to blaming those who disagree with him and pointing out why they are wrong. He channels resources toward reinforcing his position and finding people to agree and collude with him, further limiting the (potentially useful) outside information that reaches the inner circle. Together, all of these like-minded people create—instead of results—an arsenal of reasons, stories, and excuses about why they didn't or couldn't deliver.

The bottom line is, no one can guarantee a fail-proof plan. Factors like ambiguity and rapid unpredictable change make that impossible. In implementing decisions and taking action, we must remain open to new information from the marketplace and adjust our plans accordingly. When a plan isn't working, instead of the knee-jerk reaction to criticize it and decide that, because of the imperfect plan, success is out of reach, Reality-Based Leaders get their teams thinking about what they can do personally to improve the situation and how they can involve others in the solution.

The path to results, represented by the left-hand side of the circle, begins with an open mind and a willingness to face the unknown. To move team members away from judgment and toward commitment is often as simple as asking a Yes or No question: "Are you committed?" Ask for each person's declaration that they are willing to do whatever it takes (within legal, ethical bounds) regardless of role, position, or tradition. A leader who models flexibility and openness to new information above his own pride fosters those attitudes in others. Each team member is expected to make a contribution and to own responsibility for his actions. This approach yields one of two outcomes: you will get the results you sought, or you will learn something that leads you to get better results in the future. You can't lose.

> A great example of the contrast between the path to results and the path to excuses comes courtesy of Toyota dealers. Faced with a massive manufacturer recall, local dealerships across America were forced to service hundreds of cars, on short notice, within a very short period of time. The worst part? Informing their already disgruntled customers that they would have to hang around the dealership for up to two hours while the defects in their cars were being fixed.
>
> Many dealers responded by blaming the manufacturer and colluding with customers while doling out a raft of excuses for why they couldn't get the work done faster. Would you want to hear it if you were one of these dealers' customers? How likely would you be to make your next car purchase at the same dealership? The defect may have been Toyota's fault, but most dealers weren't doing anything to engender loyalty in the way they handled the problem. In subsequent years, confronted by lackluster sales, they will likely blame their poor results on consumers' loss of confidence in Toyota products.
>
> At least one dealer responded quite differently. He invited his customers to a catered dinner at his dealership while his mechanics serviced their cars, turning an inconvenient necessity into a party and making the best of a bad situation. He took personal responsibility for doing right by his customers—regardless of whose fault it was that the recall happened in the first place. Instead of blaming Toyota, he thanked his customers for their patience and, in return, I'm sure he won loyalty. I think we can predict the difference between his bottom line and his competitors' in years to come.

Limiting Belief 3: Accepting Accountability for Failures Leads to a Loss of Credibility

If you want great results and credibility, you must be willing to admit when you're wrong. Some leaders harbor a fear of admitting and discussing failures, worried that it calls their authority into question or makes them look foolish. (Often this is because they have contributed to a culture in which to admit mistakes is to be persecuted.) Contrary to what you might believe, being accountable builds trust in your leadership and increases people's confidence not only in you, but in what they themselves are willing to try. The only way accounting for your failures can hurt your credibility as a leader is if you fail to change your behavior based on what you have learned. If you want your team to learn from their mistakes, rather than cover them up out of fear or reprisals, you go first by modeling that behavior.

As challenges appear, those on the path to results don't blame, bolster their position, and make excuses. They respond with integrity and courage, accounting for the choices and actions that are currently leading to their poor outcome. The conversation becomes less about whose butt is on the line and more about choices—past and future. When you change the conversation, you gain the freedom that accompanies "response-ability"—the ability to respond differently. Responsibility opens up a grand arsenal of talent, agility, responsiveness, risk mitigation strategies, and high-quality individual contribution.

This does not just apply to the big decisions and events in an office. It's the small things, too. Imagine that you tell all of your direct reports that you need to be out of the office by 5:00. One of them has something he needs to discuss with you, but instead of bringing it up in a timely way, he procrastinates until 4:55 before calling and then, when you ask, "Can it wait until tomorrow?" he decides you are being unsupportive and feels undervalued and powerless. If he is truly accountable for his actions, however, he will be able to admit to himself that when he procrastinates, minimizes, and leaves you no time to respond, it is his behavior that leads to your unsatisfying response. The next time, he will behave differently and feel empowered and supported as a result. Small decisions and interactions like these add up over time and contribute to a better office culture for everyone.

In Part One, you learned why personal accountability is the root of all happiness and engagement in life. You owe it to your people to expect nothing less. Agility and accountability will get you great results with low stress most of the time. But if you don't get the results you seek right away, at the very least you will learn something that will show you how to better your results in the future. You will start to see your employees make amazing contributions because they know they are not going to be blamed or punished when they make mistakes—as long as they account for them honestly and commit to applying their newly acquired knowledge. Once they know that the worst thing that can happen is that they are going to learn something, it opens doors for them. Accountability is the opposite of blaming and colluding, and it's the best way to ensure that you, your people, and your business continue to grow.

Individual commitments and contributions are vitally important to getting results. That's why I have never been a proponent of the business-book cliché that is next on my list of limiting beliefs.

Limiting Belief 4: There Is No I *in* Team

I often hear leaders reminding their teams that "There is no *I* in *team*." Like much of the classic leadership advice you've been given over the years, this belief simply doesn't get results and can even lead to conflict. The way I see it, the lack of *I* is precisely the problem with teams these days. We have the worst of both worlds: maybe no one is ostentatiously taking credit, but behind the scenes, everyone is still allowed to think that he worked harder than others and can shirk responsibility for mediocre results. Regardless of whether it is openly discussed, people spend a great deal of time colluding with coworkers about who is accountable—energy that could be put to better use improving their own attitude and performance. There may not be an *I* in the word *team* but there certainly is an *I* in *win*! And in *productivity*, *improvement*, and *competition*.

Leaders need to set clear expectations and goals and focus the energy of the team on working toward the desired results. Learning and results will come only when each team member is able to assess his results honestly, without using the circumstances as an excuse. The team either hit the mark or it didn't, and it's important for each individual to account for his actions, assumptions, behaviors, and choices that contributed to the shortcomings of the team. Only by directly acknowledging what *I* did to contribute can a team member know exactly how he needs to change to create better outcomes in the future. The other benefit of this is that strong team players get the credit they deserve, which is highly motivating and plays into your "work with the willing" strategy. When people are recognized for their specific contributions to a team effort, their sense of ownership carries over into their future efforts and inspires others.

Here are the steps Reality-Based Leaders take to foster individual accountability in a team:

1. *Reality-Based Leaders make their expectations of the team very clear.*

Team projects should be approved and resources allocated based upon a business case that outlines what results are necessary to justify the investment. Do not allow the team to rewrite the business case when the going gets tough or they need to justify their choices.

2. *Reality-Based Leaders assess a team's results honestly.*

If the team nailed it, they celebrate and reward not just the team but the individual contributions to that success. But if the team did not reach the mark, they withhold credit and applause for "effort" and refrain from pointing to the circumstances as justification of shortcomings. Teams need to learn to succeed in spite of their circumstances—that is the value they add, mitigating the risks of the circumstances while implementing and executing with excellence.

3. *Lead the team through a thorough accounting of their individual contributions to the results.*

If the team had great results, ask each member to account for the decisions, choices, approaches, and behaviors that led to success so that they can intentionally duplicate them in the future. If the team's results were lackluster, ask each member to identify ways in which he personally contributed. Their responses must begin with strong "I statements" that reflect their accountability, such as "I chose," "I denied," "I assumed," "I did," "I didn't," and "I acted." Once each individual can identify his specific contributions, positive and negative, he can commit to what he will do differently next time, facilitating individual development and better future results.

Questions to Ask When Accounting for Results

- What were your results? Did you succeed or not? (Watch out for the individual or team lowering the standard, wanting to believe that they "did pretty well considering the circumstances," like they should get extra points for challenges.)
- What happened? (Listen for their stories. Are they closely accounting for the facts and their behavior?)
- How do you account for your results? (Listen for *I*, not *we* or *they* or *you*.)
- What did you believe?
- How did that belief affect your behavior, attitude, creativity, and choices?
- What were the facts? What did you know or what do we know for sure?
- How committed were you? How bought-in were you?
- What could you change to ensure your success in the future? (Listen to make sure that changes are in the first person, and not about having more resources, changing others, or changing their reality and circumstances.)
- What are you committing to in the future? (Have the person write it down—that is her new development plan—and then hold her to it.)

If you are one of those who fell for and perpetuated the idea that "there is no *I* in *team*," it's time to turn it around. Don't be afraid to challenge the conventional wisdom.

Limiting Belief 5: "Don't Bring Me a Problem Without Also Coming Armed with a Solution!"

Each and every day I work with leaders to try to help them understand that much of what they have come to accept as best practices in leadership philosophy are not only untrue but keep them from creating far greater results in their organizations.

While facilitating an assimilation session between a new leader and his team, I cringed when he started to recite this worn-out philosophy about not raising a problem without also coming armed with a solution. I know his goal was to prevent employees from whining and to encourage their willingness to help fix the problem at hand—but if this is the case, wouldn't it be more direct to tell people, "Stop whining and start helping"?

Instead of stopping the whining (which simply goes underground, adding to the drama in the workplace), this belief keeps many issues and risks from being identified at all. There are times when, by insisting that the one who identifies an issue must single-handedly recommend a workable solution, leaders are asking the impossible in today's complex and multidisciplinary team environment. In fact, this idea has stopped communication in many organizations and has led employees to believe that they can have no real impact short of inventing the total solution for any issue in their jobs.

Let's take a look at three reasons why you should put this belief to rest once and for all.

Reason 1: Employees are smart, bright people who won't bring you the issues they are capable of solving on their own—that would be wasting management resources.

Many employees are willing, bright, intelligent people who do solve issues within their locus of control as they see them arise. If you're practicing Reality-Based Leadership, you're coaching them to do just that. So it's ludicrous for a leader to tell them not to bring an issue forward without also having a solution at hand. It also hurts your credibility as someone who is in touch with the current work environment. At that moment, employees are thinking, "If I could have, I would have..." solved the problem, that is. You should certainly expect employees to be proactive and do what they can to come up with a solution, but it's important for them to recognize when to call in reinforcements—and not to fear repercussions or blame when they do so.

Reason 2: Individuals identify issues and cross-functional teams solve problems.

Most problems in business today are simply bigger than the individual and beyond the scope of his or her knowledge. But individuals— especially your customer-facing people—are great at identifying chronic problems that need solving. For example, imagine the manager of a chain drugstore that keeps running out of a best-selling product. He is not an expert on national distribution, and it's highly likely that if he is having the problem, other stores in the chain are similarly afflicted. The chain needs to assemble a team of people with that expertise to get to the bottom of the problem.

Individual employees have front-row seats on work issues—they experience the pain directly or witness the pain of the customer. Most problems are the result of flawed processes. Problems are best solved by teams who can work cross-functionally to collect data, analyze the situation, make recommendations for change, and identify risks posed by the new processes, along with mitigation strategies. So for those larger issues that an employee deems big enough to involve management (ones that require a team of experts to help), hearing his leader mouth the platitude, "Don't bring me an issue without a solution," only breeds cynicism and sarcasm. At that point, the employee is thinking, "If I could solve it single-handedly, I would, and then I would go on the circuit and talk about my amazing talents and ideas rather than work here."

Solutions to our current problems will quickly evolve into tomorrow's problems, especially if the solutions arise from a single perspective. Using a team to develop solutions, separate from the process by which an individual raises the alarm, will make the solution relevant for a little longer—perhaps even a lot longer.

Reason 3: A successful organization is full of employees who bring issues to the attention of the greater group early and without fear of reprisal.

Early in every Godzilla movie, at least one brave individual comes forward, warning of what will happen in the future when the cute, seemingly harmless little lizard grows up and destroys Tokyo. This person is usually ignored or berated. Lo and behold, ignoring the risk early on (when it would have been so easy to mitigate) results in having to call out the National Guard and the best heroes that B-movies can buy. Disallowing employees to bring in issues without solutions ensures that your organization won't have early warning of problems when they're small and relatively easy to fix. Instead, problems will become monsters before you find out about them.

Reality-Based Leaders do not damage their credibility by perpetuating the ridiculous notion that employees should not ever bring forward a problem without also having a solution at hand. Instead, insist that employees look greedily for improvement opportunities, that they fix the issues they can without causing havoc for others, that they raise their hands early while the little monster is still cute and small, and that they always show up willing to help with developing great solutions and mitigating the risks of the average short-term fix.

Limiting Belief 6: There Is No Such Thing as a Stupid Question

This is a corollary to "Everyone's opinion counts" and a big one for the current generation of leaders, who aspire to be well meaning and inclusive instead of autocratic and dictatorial. This arises from good intentions, but if you examine this statement, it is completely irrational. It might have been true for a short while when you were five and your teacher was a big, scary person and your confidence a little shaky. Teachers use this statement to encourage everyone to participate in class. When we are grown, it should be a core expectation that we all participate and choose our questions wisely.

In fact, to ask any question, uncensored, can be irresponsible. A stupid question can command meetings, research, analysis, and discussions that are a total waste of time, talent and focus, costing the company thousands of dollars. Key resources are wasted seeking an answer that doesn't exist, doesn't matter, or reinforces the erroneous belief that others are the source of our problems.

Then why does this belief, that "there are no stupid questions," live on? Too many leaders repeat it in a measly attempt to get their employees feeling comfortable and to encourage employees to ask any question any time. These same leaders lament that their people focus on the wrong things, that there is too much conflict and drama in their workplaces, and that they are not getting the results they are after. They don't realize that this is their own doing in giving employees free reign to question. It is the leaders' own fault that they are pulled away from their work by continual interruptions—usually from employees asking, "Do you have a minute?" followed by a stupid question such as "Why do things keep changing?" or "Why doesn't anyone tell me anything?" or "Who thought of this?" In his book, *QBQ! The Question Behind the Question,*[1] John Miller calls these Really Stupid Questions. I couldn't agree more—here's why:

- There is no answer to these questions. Really.
- Even if you could speculate an answer, it adds no value to the situation.
- They all imply blame.
- They fly in the face of personal accountability as a concept, let alone a core expectation.
- They are focused on other people who, last I checked, are outside of the control of the employee.

How do you know a stupid question when you hear it? A question that begins with *Why, Who,* or *When* is pretty suspect, especially if it concerns human behaviors. The words *why, who,* and *when* are only valuable when they begin questions that seek information on a process or logistical detail of a plan. When you hear yourself or someone else asking one of these stupid questions, move quickly to help steer their efforts into asking smarter questions: ones with real answers that lead to actions that truly deliver results.

People can't develop from a mindset of entitlement or victimhood. How do you get them asking better questions? John Miller has developed a great coaching method that helps people to own their accountability by asking better questions.

Say Brian has come to you, complaining, "Why doesn't Sarah ever give me the information I need to do my job?" A manager would jump in and do conflict resolution between Brian and Sarah. But you are a leader, so you focus on Brian because he is the person in front of you. You say something like, "Brian, a question of why someone does or doesn't do something tends to lead to blaming, and that isn't a great use of our time. Let's rewrite that question." The QBQ method is to rewrite a question that begins with *Why* or *Who* with *What* or *How*. So, "Why doesn't Sarah ever give me the information I need to do my job?" becomes "What can I do to get the information I need from Sarah?" or "How can I get the information I need from Sarah?" "Why do these policies keep changing?" becomes "How can I get really good at handling policy changes so that they don't seem so difficult?" or "What can I do to limit the impact of policy changes on my attitude?"

Those are profoundly different questions that come from an entirely different mindset. QBQ engages creative thinking and directs people back to their own accountability. The person in front of you stops thinking of himself as a constant victim of what comes at him from outside and starts focusing on how he can cultivate resilience and have a positive impact on the situation through his actions and his attitude.

And once he is in that mindset of accountability, we are back to the question: "Regardless of what has gone before, what would be the most valuable thing I could do right now?" Eventually, you want people to be able to go straight to that question on their own without having to run to you for guidance. They can use their energy instead to come up with breakthrough ideas and strategies for improvement and innovation.

The last limiting belief I explore in this chapter has been particularly relevant to my clients in recent years. It's one that stems from an admirable sense of responsibility on the part of leaders, but nevertheless it can have disastrous results. If you are a less experienced leader, or one who has not suffered through economic downturns before, you'll want to be very vigilant about this one.

Limiting Belief 7: In a Downturn, It's Best to Hold Back and Wait for Clarity Before You Act

If your first instinct in uncertain times is to hunker down and discontinue all the basic actions necessary to move business forward—producing, implementing, innovating, spending money, traveling, hiring, training, rewarding, and so on—until you can be more certain or gather more information and shore up resources, you are not alone. Stopping in our tracks feels safe and feeds into a widespread illusion that we should wait for clarity before we act.

If you examine what we know about survivors, however, the weakness of that position becomes abundantly clear. Survivors—of plane crashes, wars, natural disasters, and similar uncontrollable events—are rarely the ones who chose to play it safe or wait for instructions. Survivors usually report that they committed to surviving, made a plan in their minds, and acted on that plan. Waiting for clarity, in cases like these, can mean certain death. In business, we may not be facing life or death situations, but the rule still applies.

Don't wait for a return to simpler times; they're over. It is easy to adopt a mindset of retreat, but Reality-Based Leaders work instead to maintain the footprint of their businesses, and the mindset of progress and innovation, while conserving resources. A true leader understands that not making a decision is, in itself, a decision and is under no illusion that postponing will prolong the status quo.

Here is how to resist the urge to retreat and keep your teams moving forward. Cutting back should not mean holding back; instead it's about focus. The clarity you and your team are seeking is not clarity of "What should we do next?" but "What is it that we are trying to create?" To get your team staged for success, first communicate a clear and compelling vision about what is possible.

Every business book points to the importance of vision, but they fail to mention the single most important aspect of this idea: if your vision only excites those who stand to benefit personally, it is not a true vision. At best, a self-serving vision is an emotional bribe. At worst, it's an anti-incentive that saps people's motivation. Call people to greatness by making the vision about something bigger than any of you. Make it about serving, about creating a better world for your customers. But most of all, keep it alive and long term. In order to survive and thrive, team members need something to believe in—not only the possibility but the real probability of success. Work on building their confidence in the future and, most important, in their ability to deliver that future. The majority of your time should be spent managing the energy of your team—getting them to focus and refocus on efforts that have a positive impact on their reality rather than on thoughts that offer no return on investment.

Many leaders mistakenly believe that action follows clarity and inspiration, when in fact it is action itself that generates inspiration and leads to further clarity. Reality-Based Leaders insist on action. Clarity will come to you through action, followed by reflection. The risks inherent in moving forward with a "good enough" plan rather than a "perfect" plan can be mitigated by talented people who are clear about what they are trying to create, have bought into that vision, and are accountable to ensure that their customers do not feel any effects from

123

the plan's imperfections. Move forward but listen to your customers even more than before, entering into an iterative process of feedback and adaptation. Reality-Based Leaders and their teams eradicate the "I know" mindset and open themselves up to new information that allows for growth, learning, and real-time improvement of their plans.

CY'S BOTTOM LINE	It is nearly always action—not opinion—that adds the most value.

This chapter's bottom line is one of the most important ideas that I hope you will take away from this book. Chapter Eight continues the theme of returning results to the workplace, as I show you how Reality-Based Leaders create higher-functioning teams. No matter how committed you are personally, you can't get results alone or with a team that is in conflict. Instead of getting involved in conflict resolution (a waste of time), you can stop conflict before it starts.

8

Stop Judging and Start Helping

The Golden Rule of Teamwork

In this final chapter, I give you the ultimate Reality-Based guide to preventing and resolving conflict within teams. I offer strategies that will work whether you are the leader or a member of a low-functioning team. If you have ever contemplated sending your people on a team-building course or a costly off-site, save yourself a lot of effort by teaching them one key question instead: "How can I help?" This question, and the spirit in which it is asked, are the heart and soul of a healthy group dynamic. In most offices, both the question and the attitude are all too rare.

My research has led to extraordinary revelations about the roots of conflict—in particular, the morale-sapping and productivity-killing kind that develops within teams. You know what I'm talking about. You assign a group to a project, and the next thing you know, World War III has broken out in your conference room. Or people start knocking on your door to complain about one another. Or you observe that one or two people are carrying the whole effort and running themselves into the ground, getting more resentful and burned out by the day, while the rest of their so-called team orders pizza and surfs the Internet.

125

Teams in conflict cost millions of dollars a year in lost productivity and generate untold ill will among coworkers. With the help of an assistant, I embarked on an eighteen-month research project. We first surveyed teams at Mercy Medical Center in Sioux City, Iowa, then expanded the survey to the for-profit computer company Gateway, Inc., and later to nonprofit boards. We started by asking ten existing teams within each organization to rate their level of internal conflict. From each pool of ten, we chose the three teams with the highest levels of self-reported conflict to take part in our research, reserving the lower-conflict teams as control groups. We asked our high-conflict teams (nine in total) to identify the source of their conflict. Nearly 100 percent of them said that the main problem was other people.

Two root causes emerged from these conversations. The first root cause of conflict that people reported was personality clashes: that some people are difficult to work with. They're jerks, basically. The second root cause of conflict that people identified was that some people on their teams—although perfectly nice—just had no idea what they were doing. For the sake of simplicity, let's call them idiots. (You will already be familiar with jerks and idiots from your commute—jerks are the ones driving faster than you, and idiots are the ones driving slower than you.) Let me back up a moment: in all fairness, it is completely human, and natural, that when we meet someone new, within minutes we try to label them. We want to know: Does this person like me? (Is this person like me?) Do we agree? When we find someone who agrees with us, we label them immediately. (We call those people geniuses.) And when we meet somebody who does not agree with us, very quickly we have to figure out whether the person is a jerk or just kind of . . . flawed in some way. So, it's not at all strange that we heard people attributing conflict to the personalities and incompetence of others.

There's only one problem with this theory that the roots of conflict are personal: it sets up a paradigm in which there is no real solution. If the root causes of conflict could be reduced to jerks and idiots, then

126

there would have to be a way to nicen up jerks and smarten up idiots. I'm not sure if you have ever tried that, but my attempts have not been very successful. My assistant and I would ultimately find a truth more heartening than that. There was indeed a way to help teams resolve conflict, but we had to dig deeper to find it.

Ambiguity Is the Source of All Conflict

We solicited more information from the groups in conflict, asking them to rate their levels of clarity around three categories of work: their team's goals, roles, and procedures. We asked the same of our control groups. We found that the teams in conflict had much higher levels of ambiguity in all three categories. I developed a theory at that point: that this ambiguity might be the problem. To test it further, I worked with the teams to facilitate clarifying discussions about their goals, roles, and procedures. Finally, after six months, I retested the self-reported levels of conflict and found them to be much lower in all groups.

My theory was correct. The root cause of conflict is very rarely personality or incompetence. The breakthrough understanding that resulted from this research is that most conflict comes from ambiguity.

There are three basic types of ambiguity that can derail a team. First is ambiguity about goals—a lack of alignment or a lack of clarity that causes people to work against each other without realizing it. The second ambiguity is about roles. When people don't have a clear understanding of who is doing what, and where the boundaries between roles are, it leads to conflict. Finally, there is ambiguity about procedures—a lack of agreement as to how to get the work done. When we operate in this state of nonalignment, it's no wonder we judge each other as jerks and idiots. That's why, when we work with other people, we really have to get clear on what we want to create, what each person's role is, and how we are going to proceed. Those questions drive much more professional conversations, prevent conflict, and move us toward our ultimate goal a lot more efficiently.

127

Ambiguity About Goals

Think about how your staff's lack of clarity on goals affects your organization. I guarantee you that some of your people have no idea what your main goals are or how their efforts can fit in and support those goals. You have to tell them. Never take for granted that everyone is on the same page. At times, you will have to negotiate with other teams or departments to coordinate your goals in a way that's respectful of everyone's time, expertise, and effort. (Remember how the referring physicians accommodated the lab director—and vice versa—in the example in Chapter Six?)

I was called in to a financial processing firm to deal with a conflict between a leader and his team. He was a hard-driving man with a mission: to increase sales. That was what he had been hired to do. The problem, he thought, was his people. They wanted to leave at 5:00 every day, they routinely asked for time off to go to their kids' school events, they never checked their e-mail over the weekend, and they were always going on vacation. He was at his wit's end trying to succeed with this team.

The team felt that their leader was the problem. He was always calling them on the weekends, he was unsympathetic to their desire for work-life balance, and he never made an effort to connect with them on a personal level. I was a bit surprised. After all, each of them had been hired to sell, and tough bosses with high expectations are nothing new.

The source of the problem became clear to me when I spoke to the company's Human Resources Department. Their goal was employee satisfaction, and to that end, they had been recruiting using a family-friendly message that gave new hires the impression that their management would be flexible and supportive of a good work-life balance.

The lack of alignment of the leader's goal, the employees' goal, and Human Resources' goal meant that no one was happy. The employees were calling HR with complaints (the phrase "bait and switch" came up a lot) and the company's sales goals were not being met. Once we realized that this was the source of conflict, we were able to work out a solution. HR changed its recruiting strategy, and the Sales Department got a whole new compensation structure, in which those who sold the most stood to make generous commissions. The existing employees were welcome to stay and make their own decisions about how hard to work, knowing that their pay would reflect their efforts. Before long, the leader had an influx of new people who were as hard-driving as he was, and sales numbers were way up.

Ambiguity About Roles and Procedures

The same kinds of conflicts erupt around roles and procedures. We all make assumptions about what other people should be doing or what their roles encompass. But instead of discussing our expectations with them, we usually save it for the agenda after the meeting, talking about them only after they have left the room. In addition to being unfair, it's unproductive. Many of us, in order to avoid having to talk to or confront each other, look to job descriptions. But these are not fixed—they're always changing, and people's interpretations vary. So making assumptions leads to conflict, whereas talking about roles ensures that everyone is in alignment. When roles and procedures are transparent, teams run much more smoothly and efficiently.

Exercise: Management Assimilation

When a new manager comes in, even an established team can descend into conflict.

A hospital nursing unit had hired a new leader to replace their head nurse. The new hire was not a nurse herself, although she had a lot of leadership experience. The nurses were not impressed. They felt that their manager should be able to jump in and help out during busy times and vet their work for quality. They had been used to receiving that support from their previous supervisor. The new head of nursing was frustrated because she felt underutilized and could not interest the nurses in her vision for the future of their department.

In a situation like this, the best way to stop conflict in its tracks is to conduct a management assimilation. You have the prospective leader and the team sit down—separately—and define one another's roles, making a list of the qualities and abilities they expect and hope for in a leader and team. There will inevitably be gaps between the two lists. You then have the opportunity to fill those gaps, whether through compromise or enhanced job descriptions, and stop conflict based on roles and procedures before it starts.

When you look at strategies like management assimilation, avoiding conflict seems so easy. And it is. Once leaders learn to facilitate clarity around goals, roles, and procedures, and people get used to initiating those conversations, they can't understand why they had conflict at all. So why don't people come to it intuitively? Why does conflict keep happening? This is a question I am asked all the time.

It takes a lot of courage to ignore our visceral emotions and instead have a professional, clarifying conversation. It's easier in the moment to come up with a story to justify not taking the initiative: we just tell ourselves it wouldn't make any difference, because other people are unreasonable or incompetent. But the moment we make it personal, we are no longer dealing with reality. And when we start making decisions out of that kind of story, it becomes a self-fulfilling prophecy. If I see someone as a jerk, I only collect evidence that proves my point. That story feels safer than stepping up and providing real leadership: having to clarify, to reach out, to communicate, to empathize and respond. In the long run, though, it's much easier and more efficient to have that honest conversation than to live with long-term conflict. When you finally figure that out, it is life changing.

We tend to think that clarity is a byproduct of a highly functioning team, but it's the reason why they function well. Knowing this changes a leader's role in conflict. As a Reality-Based Leader, you do not have to resolve conflict—just provide clarity about goals and roles. Clarity gives employees the freedom to operate within their roles and be as effective as possible. And it stops conflict in its tracks.

Communicate consciously. Make sure everything you are asking people to do ties back into a strategic plan that you have shared with them. Never assume people will fall into place. If you are a leader at the managing director or vice president level, you should be spending 80 percent of your time with people clarifying goals and roles. If you are doing your job correctly, you should not—brace yourself—have to get involved in procedures at all. People who are clear on their goals and roles should—and will—devise their own procedures for getting the job done.

It pays to be flexible about procedures when the overall goal is being accomplished. I've seen many cases in which this was true, but perhaps none so clear-cut as the case following.

An agricultural loan company was considering firing one of its highest producers. Hank spent his days going around to farms in his pick-up truck, making loans to farmers for an agricultural loan company. He was great at connecting with the farmers, and they really trusted him. So, what was the problem?

In a word: paperwork. Hank wasn't getting it done on time. His coworkers back at the office had been putting up with it for years, and they had had enough. Hank's boss had emphasized the importance of this part of his job many times, and although he hated to let his best salesman go, it was getting too difficult to deal with the conflict in-house. High-producing or not, Hank was clearly in the wrong. He was ignoring part of his job description.

What side would you come down on if you were Hank's boss? It all depends on what's really important to you. If Hank were only an average salesperson, it would be an easy call—why keep a mediocre performer who won't do paperwork? But Hank's boss ultimately decided Hank's selling abilities were the most important value he added to the company. Instead of getting fired, Hank got a secretary to ride shotgun in the truck for $10 an hour, completing the paperwork on his hundreds of thousands in revenues.

CY'S BOTTOM LINE Clarity is the source—not the product—of a highly efficient and successful team.

Delegation Is Vital to Good Leadership

This goes back to the difference between managing and leading introduced in Chapter Four. In general, we as leaders are very comfortable talking about procedures because it gives us the great feeling of competence that got us promoted in the first place. In fact, when I attend meetings, I see most of the effort and time spent on clarifying procedures. When I notice leaders involved on this level, it is always a huge warning sign for me that they're over-managing and under-leading.

Now, many of you are saying, "That's impossible. My staff needs constant guidance. This workforce of today just isn't motivated enough, and they aren't independent and they aren't going out of their way to predict potential problems." I've heard all of the complaints. If people are that dependent on you, it's your doing and it's time to stop second-guessing them and give them some independence. This is where delegation comes in.

I'm always surprised by the amount of resistance out there when it comes to delegation. The bottom line about delegation is, when you retire from your company or when you leave your position, it is too late to be thinking about succession. Every year, your job ought to look completely different because you have developed, promoted from within, and made people more capable. If you're not growing, your people can't grow either.

Delegation doesn't mean simply pawning your work off on other people who are already as busy as you are. Rather, it's a vital aspect of leadership. Here's how to delegate to maximize your time and empower your employees:

- *Think ROI (Return on Investment).* Manage your time and resources—and those of your organization—by asking yourself, "Is this truly the best use of my time and talent, or is there a less expensive way to get this task completed?" Delegate anything that you would not pay yourself your own salary and benefits to accomplish. A vice president making her own copies for the sake of appearing an equal member of the team is a gross misuse of resources.
- *Think development.* Have a development plan in place for each of your direct reports, and delegate with an eye toward each person's growth potential. Ask yourself which person could learn and benefit

132

most from the assignment. Use delegation as an opportunity for your people to develop new skill sets and confidence.

- *Think strengths.* Ask yourself if you are truly the best person to perform the work or if there is someone stronger in that area who could do it better. Tap into the strengths of others and swap work for what plays into your strengths.

- *Think outside of your staff.* Is this work you can delegate to your customers? Can they provide the information needed? Is this work you can delegate to other departments or project teams? Often work can be delegated outside your team with great success.

- *Avoid setting others up to fail.* Delegate as quickly as you can so the individual has ample time to complete the task. Too often, we wait until the last minute to ask others for help, leaving them at a disadvantage.

- *Avoid dumping.* Connect delegation to employees' individual development plans so they see a personal benefit in tackling the work. Otherwise, they only see the benefit of your getting it off your own plate.

- *Avoid delegating unprocessed work.* Prior to delegating, ask yourself if the work can be eliminated or automated. Ask yourself, "What exactly is required?" Then you can be very clear on what the next action truly is prior to passing it on—and you can communicate that well to someone else.

- *Avoid micromanaging.* Clearly define expectations, set up predefined progress checkpoints, and use the time you free up to get other things done. Resist the urge to meddle; it is no longer your work.

- *Avoid confusion and frustration.* Inform others that you have not only delegated the task to another but have delegated the authority to them as well. Refrain from stepping in or playing the middle-man.

- *Delegation is a reward for a job well done.* Do not delegate to people with performance issues or who lack drive and ambition to succeed. If someone has not mastered his own job, address that problem using

133

the techniques from Chapter Five before you try to develop him through delegation.

For those self-described control freaks who hate to delegate because they're worried that no one else will do as good a job, I repeat: Conflicts are rarely about personality or incompetence. If someone has not lived up to your expectations, it's usually because you haven't communicated them adequately in the first place. People are not mind readers. Don't get hung up on procedures when delegating. If expectations are clear, in most cases people will have their own way of fulfilling them, and that should be fine with you.

If your employees have very clear goals and very clear roles, they will be able to design procedures that are as good as—or far better than—anything you can imagine. The more you clarify goals and roles, the less conflict you have and the less you have to manage because once people have that clarity, they can do some amazing things.

Up to now, you may have spent a lot of your time refereeing conflict. You now have a new job description: facilitator of clarity. It might take a while before you perfect this new competency. You will know when you stop getting those "Do you have a minute?" visitors knocking on your door. In the meantime, remember the techniques you have learned for refocusing individuals on personal accountability and valuable contributions, instead of fantasizing about how things "should" be.

Challenge People to Find the Lesson

My go-to strategy with a team is to insist that people assign positive motives rather than negative motives to the actions of their coworkers. In essence, I invite them to give their coworkers the benefit of the doubt, helping them to redirect the energy they are tempted to spend on their stories, complaints, and defenses to more productive activities such as learning, self-mastery, innovation, and finding creative ways forward. Reality-Based Leaders never entertain complaints about coworkers. All it does is encourage further complaint and collusion. I always tell people that the minute you start judging is the very minute you quit leading, serving, and adding value. When you're in judgment, you are dealing with your story—not with reality.

Challenge people to find the lesson instead of judging. Rather than begrudging the fact that the universe gave them, for example, a flighty, ill-prepared or micromanaging supervisor, welcome them to their next lesson in reality, which is learning to manage up. Figure out what the lesson is and get them busy mastering the necessary competency. If someone is struggling, it is not our role to judge. It's our role to ask, "How can I help?" and do everything we can to add value. This focus on results will move the team forward instead of trapping it in conflict.

This brings us to another way in which people tend to judge, which doesn't help. Researchers have identified "trust issues" as a reason for lack of results in the workplace.[1] A statistic I have seen is that employees who trust their senior management bring back 108 percent value to their shareholders, whereas employees who do not trust their senior executives only bring 66 percent back to their shareholders.[2]

What the research didn't ask is whether trust is generated by the senior executives' actions or by the employees' choices. Many of the current theories and seminars on "Trust in the Workplace" are based upon a flawed premise about the origins of trust. Here's the reality check: Trust is not something people earn; it is a choice that people make based upon their faith in their own competencies and abilities. It has little to do with the leader and everything to do with the individual team members.

135

| CY'S BOTTOM LINE | **Trust is a choice.** |

"Creating trust" is a tall order for leaders and an unacceptable excuse for the lack of results in the workplace. While leaders certainly have a responsibility to act with integrity, consistency, decency, and respect, I can guarantee you every leader will stumble at times and unwittingly fail their employees at multiple points in their relationship. That's the reality of it—they are human. If we are basing organizational profit on the perfection of our managers, it is a fragile prospect indeed.

Profits don't come directly from higher levels of trust between leaders and employees. Profits are the result of personally accountable, bullet-proof employees who make trust a conscious decision. Reality-Based Leaders make it clear that they expect this conscious act of will from their employees, and that in turn ensures profitable results.

People who trust themselves to make good choices around others and take full responsibility for their actions have a higher level of trust in others. It has nothing to do with other people and everything to do with their own decisions.

What does this have to do with your business? Everything. Trust is about your own courage and confidence, not someone else's integrity. To adopt this new belief is to set yourself free as a leader and as an employee. While you can't control or change the behavior of others, you can take responsibility and claim accountability for your own actions and behavior. Want to improve trust in your organization? Start there. People who trust themselves, trust their leaders and the companies they work for are more profitable as a result.

When Not to Trust Someone

Trust should be your default mode in all interactions if you want to be professional. Often, when you have a distrustful feeling about someone, you can trace it to a story you are telling yourself about the person rather than to the person's words or actions. (In other words, your distrust is most likely a self-created drama that you can eliminate using the techniques you learned in Chapter Two.)

There are only a few real reasons not to trust someone:

1. The person is doing something illegal.
2. The person is violating ethical guidelines.
3. The person is acting outside of his or her licensure or authority.

If any of these is the case, by all means report it. But if not, extend the person the professional courtesy of your trust, and get busy producing results together. Work on your ability to trust yourself to do the right thing in all circumstances. Profits will no longer be dependent upon the actions of others and results will happen because of you, not in spite of you.

Get Real, Step Up, Redirect

In contentious situations, there is a lot an individual can do to bring the team back to productivity. First, remind yourself and others to be very careful of what you think you know for sure. Operating out of a judging mindset of "I know" or "I am right" effectively shuts down the potential to learn or accomplish anything. I always teach people, when communicating, to seek first to understand, then to be understood. This begins with asking more questions and making fewer statements.

When you do make statements, try to avoid absolutes and leave room for other viewpoints. If you disagree with someone, begin by finding some common ground before stating your case. Construct your response carefully: "Here's what I appreciate about your perspective . . . and here's where you've lost me.... Can you explain this aspect further?" "Here's what I agree with...and here's what I am left wondering..." This will ensure that you are not seen as an adversary. The more you try to convince someone that you are right, the less convincing you become. Asking the right questions will be more persuasive than hammering home your own point of view. The point is to cultivate a mindset of "I am trying to understand" rather than "I am right." Someone who genuinely wants to understand others' perspectives will be a trusted and valued member of any team.

Another way to build strong relationships and teams is to communicate face to face whenever possible instead of sending e-mails and memos. E-mails and memos may seem easier or faster than face-to-face conversations, but they are not the most efficient means of communication. Why? They leave your message open to interpretation in ways you cannot anticipate. When you send a memo or e-mail, you send only words, and research shows that only 7 percent of someone's understanding of a message can be accounted for by words alone. Thirty-eight percent of any message is communicated by tone of voice, and an alarming 55 percent has to do with our body language.[3] That means that 93 percent of any e-mail or memo is left to the interpretation of the recipient. Better to take a walk down the hall and be sure of how your message is received.

It is inevitable that misunderstandings and disagreements will happen among coworkers, and it is tempting and all too easy to personalize those conflicts. They hook your ego and seem like the main event when they are only a distraction. It is even easier for leaders to collude with employees in the personalizing of conflict, spending valuable time and energy listening to the stories, assigning motives, doling out wisdom, and mandating that all involved "get along." The reward for this investment of energy, innovation, and focus? Mediocrity, stagnation, and a miserable status quo. Reality-Based Leaders know that personalizing conflict is a luxury we can't afford. In times of conflict, what people need most is for you to get real, step up, redirect their energy, and help them see their circumstances differently so that they can create better professional relationships and greater results in their teams. The good news is, you already have the tools you need to do this.

Here are five steps for getting back on a positive track, using the skills you've learned from this book:

1. *Do a reality check.*

It is not conflict itself that causes us stress but the story we tell ourselves about it. Get back to the facts of the situation by editing out anything that you can't absolutely know to be true. Give others the benefit of the doubt when assigning motives. When faced with conflict, ask, "What is the next right action I can take that would add the most value to the situation?" Direct your energy on that action.

2. *Get clear about motives.*

Seek to be successful rather than right. Too many times, you may abandon organizational goals in order to achieve your own motives, such as love, approval, or appreciation. Without those motives, you can see your role more clearly and achieve the goals at hand.

3. *Be the change.*

The only thing missing in a situation is that which you, yourself, are not offering in the moment. Practice those virtues that you have determined to be lacking in others, such as open-mindedness, patience, inclusiveness, tolerance, and appreciation. Drop your double standards: stop expecting others to excel at skills you have not yet mastered.

4. *See others through a lens of love and respect—not anger and fear.*

When faced with those whose personalities are different from ours, or whose behaviors have reached a stress-induced inappropriateness, work to see through those behaviors and identify their needs or goals. Ask yourself, "What are they striving for?" Then ask, "How can I help them achieve it?"

5. *Invoke a clearer, higher perspective.*

When you sense that conflict is getting personal, be prepared to facilitate a quick return to a professional perspective by asking your team to clarify the overarching goal of their work together. A common goal is one that is inclusive and compelling to all, such as customer loyalty, increased sales, or organizational growth. Elicit the participation of each team member by asking questions such as, "Given our goal, what do you think is the best way to move forward? What is the best that you can contribute?"

Ultimately, my hope for individuals, teams, and organizations is the same: That instead of reporting the news (making doomsday predictions, complaining, trying to change their circumstances, or arguing with reality), they will make the news in a positive way—solving problems, taking advantage of opportunities, and showing courage and the willingness to be great. When we stop judging and start helping, everything becomes possible.

CONCLUSION

The Reality-Based Leader's Manifesto

In the offices where I worked before I started consulting, Human Resources directors used to get very twitchy when I talked about radical concepts like "working with the willing" and the difference between managing and leading. Now I make my living challenging conventional wisdom, and I'll tell you what: Iconoclasm is underrated in the workplace. You owe it to yourself and everyone you influence to question what you have believed to date. There is so much at stake.

In this book, I've given you some unconventional wisdom about how to strengthen your working relationships, create bullet-proof teams, and return peace, sanity, and results to your workplace. Think about this: You spend more time with your coworkers than you do with your spouse or your children. It's essential that you find a way not only to get real with these people and make the most of what can end up as some of the best years of your life. It's up to you whether your workday is an ordeal in the company of jerks and idiots or a time when camaraderie and succeeding in spite of your circumstances bring you satisfaction and profit.

If you are feeling a little uncertain at this point, you are not alone. Most of the people I work with take some time to process what they have learned. That's because, when your thinking gets interrupted, it creates cognitive dissonance. If you are feeling the effects of that, have courage: it's from that confused state that all breakthroughs come.

The great thing about life is, every day we get a new shot at it. If your office atmosphere leaves a lot to be desired, it's in your power to begin creating a better place to work, starting now, with the principles you've learned in this book.

We, as Reality-Based Leaders, . . .

1. Refuse to argue with reality
2. Greet change with a simple "Good to know"; defense is an act of war
3. Depersonalize feedback—whatever the source
4. Let go of our need for love, approval, and appreciation at work so we can focus on the goals of our organization and not on satisfying our egos
5. Are very careful about what we think we know for sure
6. Ask ourselves, "What is the next right thing I can do to add the most value?"
7. Ask others, "How can I help?" instead of judging and blaming
8. Work to find the opportunity in every challenge
9. Work harder at being happy than at being right
10. Work with the willing
11. Lead first, manage second
12. Value action over opinion

It's one thing to grasp these principles intellectually and another to apply them and ultimately make them part of your organization's DNA. I am not going to leave you out in the cold to implement them alone any more than I would leave one of my private consulting clients. We can do it together.

I have set up a Web site, www.realitybasedleadership.com, exclusively for you, the readers of this book. The password is "Ditch the Drama." By signing up, you will gain privileged access to a world of coaching resources and extra content to help you become a Reality-Based Leader, including

- A message board where you can post questions that I will answer in writing or address in my weekly Podcasts
- Access to weekly Podcasts, live and archived
- A call-in number to participate in group coaching calls
- Access to extra assessments and tests
- My Reality-Based Leadership Blog
- Audio and video recordings of my seminars
- Firsthand exposure to my latest research on the real drivers of engagement
- The opportunity to have your company participate in my newest project
- Recordings of my ongoing coaching sessions with leaders, available for you to listen in anytime
- Webinars
- Early registration to my keynote and coaching events

When you sign up, you'll be able to create a personal development plan and receive ongoing support as you work toward your goals. You'll have the opportunity to connect with a community of like-minded people who are rejecting conventional Human Resources wisdom and embracing Reality-Based Leadership. If you join our revolution, the end of this book will be just the beginning.

Early on in my career, I was charged with leading a group of students with very basic orienteering skills on a challenging hike. It was one of the first times I'd led a group, and I was more than a little worried that we would get lost in the forest. My mentor advised me that if our path forward was obscured by vegetation, hills, or other barriers, I should simply seek out the very highest point possible by climbing a tree, scaling a cliff, or hiking up a mountain. Getting to the highest point would provide a whole new view, a perspective I should then commit to memory as a roadmap once we were back on the lower, more confusing ground.

Thanks to his advice, my team returned safely from their challenge, but what I could not have anticipated at the time was that I would still be looking to this metaphor on a daily basis more than twenty years later. Today, I am convinced that our main responsibilities as Reality-Based Leaders are to help those we lead find a higher and more meaningful perspective, make sense of the suffering in their lives, and move through limiting beliefs to great results. Now more than ever, we must lead our people to a higher place so they can see their realities clearly and take the next right step toward success.

Appendixes

APPENDIX 1

Alignment Survey

It is easy to diagnose the health of individuals within an organization—the level of drama versus peace—with a simple survey. I ask individuals to circle the number that corresponds to their feelings about these nine indicators. The more low-number answers you get, the more you can be sure that you have a high level of drama, arguing with reality, and learned helplessness.

When I go into organizations that are struggling, I know that the mindset of their employees is the most reliable indicator of whether they will survive. I worked in health care for many years. When I analyzed the results of alignment surveys at hospitals and clinics, I found that—independent of all other conditions—if 30 percent or more of the surveys came up low, within three to five years that hospital or clinic was going to have major solvency problems. When people feel a lack of responsibility for their results, and they have little sense of ownership or commitment, you will have a sick organization regardless of what else you may be doing right.

Alignment Survey

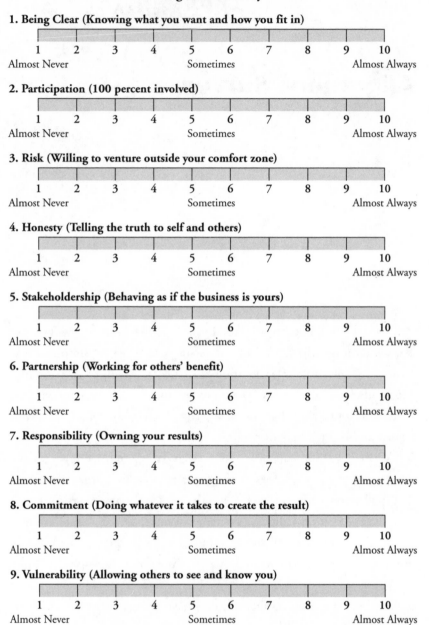

1. Being Clear (Knowing what you want and how you fit in)

| 1 | 2 | 3 | 4 | 5 | 6 | 7 | 8 | 9 | 10 |

Almost Never   Sometimes   Almost Always

2. Participation (100 percent involved)

| 1 | 2 | 3 | 4 | 5 | 6 | 7 | 8 | 9 | 10 |

Almost Never   Sometimes   Almost Always

3. Risk (Willing to venture outside your comfort zone)

| 1 | 2 | 3 | 4 | 5 | 6 | 7 | 8 | 9 | 10 |

Almost Never   Sometimes   Almost Always

4. Honesty (Telling the truth to self and others)

| 1 | 2 | 3 | 4 | 5 | 6 | 7 | 8 | 9 | 10 |

Almost Never   Sometimes   Almost Always

5. Stakeholdership (Behaving as if the business is yours)

| 1 | 2 | 3 | 4 | 5 | 6 | 7 | 8 | 9 | 10 |

Almost Never   Sometimes   Almost Always

6. Partnership (Working for others' benefit)

| 1 | 2 | 3 | 4 | 5 | 6 | 7 | 8 | 9 | 10 |

Almost Never   Sometimes   Almost Always

7. Responsibility (Owning your results)

| 1 | 2 | 3 | 4 | 5 | 6 | 7 | 8 | 9 | 10 |

Almost Never   Sometimes   Almost Always

8. Commitment (Doing whatever it takes to create the result)

| 1 | 2 | 3 | 4 | 5 | 6 | 7 | 8 | 9 | 10 |

Almost Never   Sometimes   Almost Always

9. Vulnerability (Allowing others to see and know you)

| 1 | 2 | 3 | 4 | 5 | 6 | 7 | 8 | 9 | 10 |

Almost Never   Sometimes   Almost Always

APPENDIX 2

Self-Test: Managing Versus Leading

Below are twenty-four questions—four for each of six major aspects of a leader's role. Answer each question as quickly and candidly as you are able—True or False—and keep track of your answers.

Planning

1. I invest time in planning. T/F
2. I have little time for planning ahead. T/F
3. I involve others in shaping plans. T/F
4. I tend to operate on a short-term or crisis-to-crisis basis. T/F

Goal Setting

5. I work with others to develop goals and plans to achieve them. T/F
6. When I set goals, I tend to hand them down to employees as instructions. T/F
7. I make sure that goals and expectations are always written down and clear, and they inform my management. T/F

149

8. I am more activity- and task-oriented than results- and goal-driven. T/F

Giving Performance Feedback

9. I give feedback on a regular basis and make sure to tie it into what employees are working on. T/F
10. I give feedback at annual review time. T/F
11. I provide both positive and negative feedback in a specific way so the staff always knows where they stand. T/F
12. I occasionally give praise but am more likely to give feedback when something has gone wrong. T/F

Dealing with Performance Problems

13. I address issues as they arise with a solutions-oriented approach. T/F
14. I often feel uncomfortable addressing performance problems and avoid it if I can. T/F
15. I work with employees to map out plans for improvement. T/F
16. Seeking punitive measures is often the first action I take when dealing with performance problems. That's what HR is for. T/F

Delegating

17. I delegate as much as possible to maximize resources and improve productivity. T/F
18. I tend to delegate little beyond simple tasks. T/F
19. I delegate based on staff development needs and succession plans and offer support and guidance. T/F
20. When I delegate a task, I expect staff to get on with it with a minimum of help from me. Otherwise, why delegate at all? T/F

Mentoring and Staff Development

21. I take an active interest and get involved in employee training and growth. T/F

22. I take a learn-on-your-own, sink-or-swim approach to development. T/F

23. I encourage staff to consider extra training and lateral moves within the organization when it might expand their capabilities long term. T/F

24. I am primarily concerned with staff members' performance in their current jobs, especially since these days turnover is high and we are unlikely to keep staff long term. T/F

Scoring:

1. Count the number of True responses you gave to the odd-numbered questions: _____

2. Count the number of True responses you gave to the even-numbered questions: _____

The odd-numbered questions are leadership indicators, while the even-numbered questions are correlated to management. Therefore, if your first score is anywhere from much lower than, to about equal to, your second score, you are definitely over-managing and under-leading.

If you scored high for leadership indicators, that's great news. Review your answers within each of the six aspects and see if you scored higher for management in one or more of them. This will show you the skills you most need to develop in order to lead first, manage second.

Feedback Frame

S teps 1 and 2 will help you to structure your feedback and be very specific when speaking to your employee. Step 3 allows for a constructive response on the part of the employee. Step 4 is your opportunity to discuss possibilities and next steps together.

Step 1

What is the employee doing that is working?

What does she or he do that is inspiring to me as a leader, or to the group?

Acknowledge the employee's character traits, effort, passion . . .

See through behavior to need or intent.

Affirm the person's strengths.

Step 2

What is the employee doing that is not working yet?

What are the areas in which the employee is capable but not yet consistent?

What hasn't the employee developed or fine-tuned?

What is untested or too soon to test?

What does she or he need to work on or develop next?

Step 3

Your purpose is to make sure your feedback was clear to the employee and to understand his or her thinking, level of accountability, and stories.

Invite the employee to respond with a question or statement appropriate to your feedback. Here are some possibilities:

"Help me understand your perspective."

"What is keeping you from fulfilling your commitment?"

"How are you contributing to this situation?"

Step 4

Discuss what is possible and let the employee know what support you can offer. Elicit his or her plans for development.

Can you both agree on what fluency in this skill would look like?

What are the benefits to the employee of developing in this area?

What does the employee's development road map look like?

NOTES

Introduction

1. Employee Engagement Index, *Gallup Management Journal,* 2008.

Chapter One

1. The phenomenon of learned helplessness was discovered in the 1970s by social psychologists, including Martin Seligman, who were studying depression and the effects of stress. They took three rats and separated them and put them into cubicles. Rat C was the control rat. They hooked Rats A and B to electrodes that gave them synchronized shocks at random intervals. The researchers measured the effects of this outside stress by giving each rat an escape task. They found that a little bit of stress is actually good for performance. Rats A and B performed better than Rat C. The scientists continued the experiment with random, equal shocks to Rats A and B. Later, though, Rat A was given a way to stop the shocks himself, while Rat B had no control over the shocks. Rats A and C performed well. Rat B, however, ultimately refused to attempt the task, and appeared listless. Rat A,

even though he had the same externally inflicted shocks as Rat B, had cause to believe that his actions counted, whereas Rat B did not. That was the only difference that could account for the variance in their results. Over time, through this and other experiments, the researchers developed the idea that our belief in our ability to affect our environment and our circumstances has a greater impact on our results than our actual ability.

Chapter Five

1. C. Wakeman, *Resistant Employees' Drain on Management Resources*. Omaha, NE: Clarkson College Graduate Program, 1992.
2. C. Wakeman, *Little Return on Management Time Investment in Resistant Employees*. Omaha, NE: Clarkson College Graduate Program, 1992.

Chapter Seven

1. John Miller, *QBQ! The Question Behind the Question*. New York: Putnam, 2004.

Chapter Eight

1. G. E. Bader and A. Liljenstrand, *The Value of Building Trust in the Workplace*. WorkIndex.com. A "study of 4,000 employees in eight countries concludes that building trust and emphasizing business ethics in the workplace pays off in tangible and intangible ways, helping the company's bottom line." Sponsored by United Technologies and conducted by Pamela Shockley-Zalabak, PhD, Kathleen Ellis, PhD, and Ruggero Cesaria, the study showed "trust is more than a social virtue and it serves as an economic imperative for business resilience in a global marketplace."
2. www.managementtraining.biz/management_training_Building-Trust-In-The-Workplace-with-Management-Training.html.
3. A. Mehrabian, *Silent Messages: Implicit Communication of Emotions and Attitudes*, 2nd ed. Belmont, CA: Wadsworth, 1981.

ACKNOWLEDGMENTS

I know only one thing for sure: I am the luckiest woman alive and my life is profoundly blessed with the most amazing group of souls to whom I am immensely grateful. My thanks to a few who come to mind:

Dad, thanks for the great start in life, always insisting that I stand proud and succeed regardless of my circumstances. You gave me the gift of storytelling and the gift of being loved my whole life. I am proud to be a Dorr.

Mom, you gave me a perfect example that as a woman, you really can have it all, a great family, a passion for a career, a rich life, and a ton of friends. I miss you, a lot!

George, Charles, Henry, and William, you are the most amazing sons and incredible roomies in our great big red fraternity house on the corner. I am blown away to be able to be the mother of four such strong, sensitive, loving, dedicated, supportive boys who are wise beyond your years. Thanks for keeping me humble and centered and for providing so many major distractions this year that I didn't have time to be nervous about writing a book.

George, thank you for supporting me, loving me, and blessing me in spite of our struggles. And most of all, thank you for naming me "Cy."

To my brothers and sisters, it has been a very cool thing to grow up with you and to be loved by you through all the stages of my life.

Sara, I simply adore you. You are a talented, strong, smart, up and coming force! I so appreciate the fact that you love my boys in person when I need to love them from afar. You are a great addition to the team.

Lisa, you are talented, witty, a mover of mountains, the ultimate goal fulfillment center, my Rock of Gibraltar, and a dear friend who came into my life at the perfect time—further proof that the universe is kind. I am grateful beyond words.

Giles Anderson of the Anderson Literary Agency, you are such a super-cool and hip agent and I am so grateful that I picked up that phone in Cabo! You have been a wonderful mentor and guide through this process. Thanks for hanging with me until we figured out the evasive value proposition and for hooking me up with the amazing Erin Moore and Karen Murphy. You have turned my dream into a reality in a single year. Simply put, *You rock!*

Erin Moore, my like-minded cowriter, I am blown away by your genius in turning my ideas into wonderful text. You have been the perfect partner in the creation of this book, a calming force across the ocean and a trusted guide every step of the way. I look forward to many more collaborative books to come!

Karen Murphy, Gayle Mak, and the rest of the Jossey-Bass team, I am so thrilled that you do not believe in single chances and instant rejection. Thank you for staying the course and mentoring me through the process of publishing my first book. Your editing is simply amazing—what I had envisioned as a painful process was a joy and I am thrilled with the end product. You have truly called me to the next level in my life and have done some heavy lifting along the way.

Conception and Barollio, I so appreciate all you do for me and for my family.

Doug, Sharon, and the incredible team of Ervin and Smith in Omaha, Nebraska, or "Team Wakeman" as you are known in my heart. You are the first disciples of Reality-Based Leadership, and it has been incredible to watch your success as you have wholeheartedly adopted and implemented all the techniques laid out in this book. You and your organization are proof that this stuff works. Oh yeah, and as the top PR/marketing agency in the world, thanks for making me famous!

Cathy, my beloved friend and constant growth companion, you give me clarity, vision, and faith. Dawn and Michele, my walking buddies, you have kept me loved and supported forever. Carson, my fearless friend, you always go first and then come back for me—thanks for introducing me to BK and the gang. Pam and Karla, thanks for your professional and personal support and for giving me some of my first great contracts.

Lisa, who so freely shares my favorite place on earth, Rancho Pescadero, I love you for toughening me up and helping me kick the Buddha out of my bedroom. Thanks for all the coaching and for giving the perfect oasis to both begin and conclude this book.

To the great teachers in my adult life, Steve Saunders, Travis Anderson, John Miller, and Byron Katie, I am changed because of you.

To the great teachers from my childhood, Mr. Dye for giving birth to the writer in me, Mr. Sorum for the incredible speech training, and Mrs. Houser for always believing in me.

Last, to Chuck Blomberg, Mary Dahlen, and the women at Mercy Medical Center, who taught me all I know about coaching and leading others. You gave me a great start to my professional life.

ABOUT THE AUTHOR

Cy Wakeman's background combines four successful business start-ups with eighteen years working and consulting in manufacturing, banking, government, high tech, and health care.

Cy has honed her Reality-Based Leadership philosophy as a consultant to top executives and organizations seeking to thrive in difficult times. She is a sought-after conference headliner, delivering more than 100 keynote programs annually.

Cy's clients include Woodmen of the World, Ervin and Smith, New York Presbyterian, The Society for Human Resource Management, Weil Cornell, Hewlett-Packard, Gateway, Verizon Wireless, U.S. Cellular, TD Ameritrade, First Data Resources, ConAgra, Merrill Lynch, Mars Confectionary, Omnium Worldwide, First National Merchant Solutions, Wellmark, Wells Fargo, Farm Bureau Federation, Trinity Health Systems, and the National Guard.

INDEX

A

Accountability: chaos of empowerment without, 64–65; employee survey used for, 65–67; limiting belief on credibility being tied to, 112–114; personal happiness linked to personal, 14–15; QBQ method for, 121–122; questions to ask for results, 116

Actions: based on feelings about event, 21; inspiration generated by, 123–124; learning to respond to facts and not story, 22–24; results of the, 21–22; understanding failure to act, 55–56; value of helping or coaching, 54

Adversity response, 85–87

The Alignment Survey, 46

Ambiguity: about goals, 128; as source of all conflict, 127–131

Anger: redirecting your, 140; as response, 95–96. *See also* Conflict; Feelings

"Arguing with reality": examining the appeal of, 16–18; examples of, 12–13; futility of, 62–63; Reality-Based Leaders' refusal to engage in, 33. *See also* Reality

B

Battle fatigue, 14

Behavior: ego-centric, 38–41; of favorite employees, 74; Freak-Out Factor, 16–18; identifying organizational goals from, 46; learning from feedback and changing, 44–46. *See also* Change

Being right. *See* "I am right" mindset

Beliefs: embracing reality instead of personal, 10–13; judgments based

Page references followed by *fig* indicate an illustrated figure; references followed by *t* indicate a table.

on, 10; Reality-Based Leader
facilitating changes in, 52, 75; resistant employees' retreat to safest, 84.
See also Limiting beliefs

Bullet-proofing competencies: ability to
respond to adversity, 85–86; commitment to succeed, 87–91; will to
resolve and move through conflict,
92–94

Bullet-proofing employees: best practices
during crisis, 96–101; importance
of, 83–85; three core competencies
of, 85–94; three mistakes to avoid,
94–96

Bullet-proofing mistakes: dropping support, 96; lying, 95; trying to reason
with anger, 95–96

Burnout, 92

C

Change: becoming the, 139;
bullet-proofing your employees to
handle, 83–101; commitment to
make successful, 87–88; Reality-Based
Leader facilitating belief, 52, 75;
redirecting your focus for, 72–74;
response to adversity for, 85–87;
three stages of, 82–83; *Who Moved
My Cheese?* on, 72. *See also* Behavior

Change mistakes: dropping support after
change is made, 96; lying, 95; trying
to reason with anger, 95–96

Chronic Shock Syndrome, 16

Coaching: The Alignment Survey to
prepare for, 46; by allowing people to
grow into their roles, 61–62; avoiding
blame and focusing your, 56–59; by
building confidence, 59–60; focusing
on hearts and minds, 60–61; leading
then managing principles, 53–64; on
playing favorites, 70–82; teaching
employees to reframe, 54–56; on
teamwork, 125–137

Common ground, 40–41

Competencies: ability to response to
adversity, 85–87; commitment to
succeed, 87–91; as following confidence, 59–60, 90–91; thinking inside
the box, 93–94; will to move through
and resolve conflict, 92–94

Confidence: coaching by building,
59–60; competency as coming after,
90–91; ego versus, 35–36; as leadership quality, 35

Conflict: aiming for common ground in
case of, 40–41; ambiguity as source
of all, 127–131; costs of, 126; finding solutions instead of engaging in,
41–43; moving through and resolving, 92–94; professional perspective
to resolve, 140; theory on root causes
of, 126–127. *See also* Anger; Events

Consensus builders, 38

Cortisol hormone, 60

Credibility, 112–114

Crises best practices: dealing with emer-
gencies/disasters, 99–101; dealing
with impending layoffs, 97–99

Cy's bottom lines: action, not opinion,
adds the most value, 124; bad ego day
is a good day for soul of a leader, 36;
bulletproof employees use change to
their advantage, 88; clarity is source
of a successful team, 131; happiness
correlation to personal accountability,
15; learn not to put up with problem employees, 76; over-managing is
under-leading, 64; trust is a choice,
135; what is missing from situation is
whatever you are not giving, 32–33

D

Decision making: aiming for common
ground, 40–41; ego motivation vs.
organization goals, 38*t*

Defensiveness, 39–40

Delegation: managing vs. leading and,
131–132; maximizing your time/
empowering employees by, 132–134

Depersonalizing work environment, 39

Disaster best practices, 99–101

E

Editing stories: client breakthrough by, 27–30; exercise on learning to, 25–26

Ego motivation: masquerading as self-lessness, 36–38; organizational goals versus, 38*t*

Ego-centric behaviors: defensiveness, 39–40; knee-jerk criticism, 40–41; personalizing your work, 39

Ego-centricity: confidence versus, 35–36; people pleasers as targets for, 38; warning signs of, 36–37

Einstein, Albert, 52

Emergency best practices, 99–101

Emotional blackmail: description of, 62; disregarding attempts at, 62–64

Employee survey: for accountability, 65–67; eliminating the victim factor from, 66

Employees: bullet-proofing your, 83–101; event-to-results process taken by, 19–22; Gallup poll on disengaged, 2, 3; identifying the visionaries among, 71–72; impending layoffs of, 97–99; lack of feedback as causing issues with, 76–77; learning not to put up with problem, 76; limiting belief related to solutions by, 117–119; mediocre, 70; playing favorites with, 70–82; resistance from, 79–82. *See also* Roles

Empowerment: accountability required with, 64–65; delegation for employee, 132–134

Events: action following your feelings from the, 21; description of, 20; feelings following your thinking about the, 21; finding solutions when things go wrong, 41–43; results of your reality of the, 21–22; thinking to create your version of reality of the, 20. *See also* Conflict; Problem situations

Exercises: learning to edit your story, 25–26; management assimilation, 129; thinking inside the box for solutions, 94

F

Fact-based responses, 22–24

Failure to act, 55

Feedback: employee issues caused by lack of, 76–77; Feedback Frame resource for giving, 78; learning and growing from, 44–46; negative criticism, 40–43; not everyone's opinion counts, 106–108; one-on-one meeting agenda for giving, 78–79

Feelings: action taken following, 21; following the thinking about event, 21; learning to respond to facts and not story, 22–24; result following action and, 21–22. *See also* Anger

Fight-or-fight mode, 60–61

Freak-Out Factor quiz, 16–18

G

Goals. *See* Organizational goals

Godzilla movie analogy, 119

H

Hank, 131

Happiness: personal accountability correlation to, 14–15; self-told stories eroding your, 15

Helpless stories, 24

Human Resources (HR), 3

I

"I am right" mindset: diverting energy to blame others, 111; high price of the, 41, 42; learning to redirect your, 137–140; prioritizing the, 16, 23; Reality-Based Leaders' focus on being happy vs., 142

"I know" mindset, 124, 137

Inspiration, 123–124

J

Judgments: challenging people to find the lesson instead of, 134–135; embracing reality instead of making, 10–13; getting sidetracked by villains and blame, 56–59; personal beliefs creating, 10; Steve's tendency to make, 42–43

K

Karen: editing the story breakthrough by, 27–29; situation faced by, 27; stress experienced by, 27–28
Knee-jerk criticism, 40–41

L

Layoffs, 97–99
Leadership: absence of reality-based, 2; delegation as vital to good, 131–134; Human Resources' inability to fill gap of poor, 3; management compared to, 49–50; people and circumstances as challenges of, 1–2; people work of, 50; self-testing your own, 67; under-leading form of, 50–52. *See also* Reality-Based Leadership
Leading/managing principles: 1: resist urge to add more value, 53–56; 2: coach the person in front of you, 56–59; 3: work on confidence first, and competence will follow, 59–60; 4: forget logistics and focus on hearts and minds, 60–61; 5: allow people to grow into their roles, 61–62; 6: disregard attempts at emotional blackmail, 62–64
Learned helplessness: description of, 13–14; examining the appeal of, 16–18
Limiting beliefs: 1: everyone's opinion counts, 106–108; 2: great results can only come from perfect plans, 108–112; 3: accepting accountability for failures is loss of credibility, 112–114; 4: there is no *I* in *team*, 114–116; 5: don't bring a problem without also a solution, 117–119; 6: there is no such thing as a stupid question, 119–122; 7: hold back during downturn, 122–124. *See also* Beliefs

Loyalty, 79
Lying, 95

M

Management: business work of, 50; leader's focus on resource, 51–52; leadership compared to, 49–50; over-managing/micromanaging form of, 50–52, 133; self-testing your own, 67. *See also* Leading/managing principles
Management assimilation exercise, 129
Mediocre employees, 70
Micromanaging, 50–52, 133
Miller, John, 120
Motivation: assigning positive vs. negative, 134–135; ego, 36–38*t*; getting clear about your, 139

N

Negative brainstorming, 88–90
Negative feedback: aiming for common ground instead of, 40–41; how to stop using, 41–43; learning and growing from, 44–46
No *I* in *team* belief, 114–116
No stupid questions belief, 119–122

O

Opinion: limiting belief on importance of everyone's, 106–108; value through action and not, 124
Organizational goals: ambiguity about, 128; behavior that reflects, 46; ego motivation versus, 38*t*; providing clarity about, 130–131

P

People pleasers, 38
Plans: false belief on results requiring perfect, 108–112; for transition of resistant employees, 81–82
Playing favorites: compensating value and not effort, 74–75; fairness of, 70–71; identifying the visionaries, 71–72; loyalty component of,

79; one-on-one meeting agenda for connecting, 78–79; redirecting your focus on, 72–74

Problem situations: event-to-results process in, 19–22; Godzilla movie analogy for, 119; learning and growing from feedback on, 44–46; limiting belief on employee-solutions for, 117–119; making judgments about, 10–13, 42–43; negative criticism responses vs. common ground, 40–43; reframing, 54–56. *See also* Events; Solutions

Professional courtesy, 24–25

Professional perspective, 140

Q

QBQ! The Question Behind the Question (Miller), 120

Questions: to ask resistant employees, 80–81; to ask when accounting for results, 116; belief on no stupid, 119–122; QBQ method for using, 120–122

R

Reality: commitment to succeed in new, 87–88; defensiveness against, 39–40; learning to edit the story to accept, 25–30; as a projection of you, 30–32; response to adverse, 85–87; story versus fact-based, 22–24. *See also* "Arguing with reality"

Reality check, 139

Reality-Based Leaders: characteristics of, 33; crises best practices for, 97–101; facilitating belief changes, 52, 75; inner peace movement role of, 33; leading first, managing second principles followed by, 53–64; negative brainstorming by, 88–90; playing favorites, 70–82; providing clarity about goals, 130–131; redirecting your "I am right" mindset, 137–140; resource management by,

51–52; understanding dangers of being indispensible, 51

Reality-Based Leadership: absence of, 2; delegation as vital to, 131–134; description and benefits of, 3–5; resource management focus of, 51–52; *You go first* theme of, 53. *See also* Leadership

Redirecting yourself: five steps for, 139–140; focus for change, 72–74; strategies for, 137–139

Reframing: coaching employees by helping them, 54–56; description of, 54

Resistant employees: dealing with, 79–80; negative brainstorming to transform, 88–90; planning transition of, 81–82; questions to ask, 80–81

Respect, 140

Restoring peace: measuring Freak-Out Factor to understand, 16–18; understanding source of your suffering for, 12–13

Results: learning to respond to facts and not story, 22–24; limiting belief on perfect plans required for, 108–112; process of event-to-, 19–22; questions to ask when accounting for, 116; stress created from the, 19, 21–22; Toyota dealer's example of getting, 112

Results Circle, 109–110*fig*

ROI (return on investment), 132

Roles: allowing people to grow into their, 61–62; ambiguity about procedures and, 129–131; providing management assimilation to establish, 129; Reality-Based Leaders and inner peace movement, 33. *See also* Employees

Root causes of conflict theory, 126–127

S

Self-serving vision, 123

Self-test, 67

Solutions: best practices for crises, 97–101; instead of engaging in conflict, 41–43; limiting belief on employee, 117–119; thinking inside the box for, 94–95. *See also* Problem situations

Steve, 42–43

Stories: beliefs and judgments leading to, 10; client breakthrough by learning to edit, 27–30; editing your, 25–26; embracing reality to create, 10–13; eroding your happiness through, 15; event-to-results process creating, 19–22; helpless, 24; learning to respond to the facts and not, 22–24; professional courtesy instead of reacting to, 24–25; as a projection of you, 30–32; stress resulting from created, 10, 18, 22; victim, 24, 55–56, 66; villain, 24, 56–59

Stress: beliefs, judgments, and stories leading to, 10; client breakthrough by editing story and reducing, 27–30; event-to-results process illustration, 20*fig*; process of event-to-results of, 19–22

Stupid questions belief, 119–122

Suffering: examining the real sources of, 9–10; learned helplessness creating, 13–14; measuring your office's Freak-Out Factor, 16–18; understanding the source of your, 12–13

Susan, 57–59

T

Tammy, 57–59

Teams: clarity as source of successful, 131; how ambiguity derails, 127–131; importance of delegation in, 131–134; no *I* in *team* belief about, 114–116

Thinking: action taken following feelings and, 21; creating your reality from, 20; delegation strategies through, 132–134; event leading to, 19–20; feeling that following mental work of, 21; results taken from created reality, 21–22

Thinking inside the box, 93–94

Trust: as a choice, 135; issues related to creating, 136; value of creating, 136; when not to trust someone, 137

V

Value: action, not opinion, adds the most, 124; of coaching actions, 54; compensate employee, 74–75; of creating trust, 136; resist urge to add more, 53–56

Victim stories: description of, 24; eliminated as employee survey factor, 66; taking responsibility and avoiding, 55–56

Villain stories: coaching while avoiding, 56–59; description of, 24

Vision: limiting belief on waiting for clarity of, 122–124; pitfall of self-serving, 123

Visionary employees, 71–72

W

Wakeman, George, 11–12

Who Moved My Cheese? (Johnson), 72

"Work with the willing" strategy, 115

Y

You go first theme, 53